P9-COP-836

WESTWARD HO!

Somerset Valley
School Library
45 Blake St
Hartland, Maine

DISCARD

DISCARD

WESTWARD HO!

An Activity
Guide to the Wild West

Laurie Carlson

CHICAGO
REVIEW
PRESS

Somerset Valley
School Library
45 Blake St
Hartland, Maine

For Brian, with love.

Library of Congress Cataloging-in-Publication Data
Carlson, Laurie 1952–
Westward ho! : an activity guide to the Wild West / Laurie
Carlson. — 1st ed.
p. cm.
Includes bibliographical references.
Summary: Provides historical details of the settlement of the West and descriptions of frontier life with accompanying activities.
ISBN 1-55652-271-1
1. West (U.S.)—Social life and customs—Study and teaching—
Activity programs—Juvenile literature. [1. West (U.S.)—Social
life and customs. 2. Frontier and pioneer life.] I. Title.
F596.C25 1996
978'.02—dc20   96-10841
                                                    CIP
                                                    AC

©1996 by Laurie Carlson
All rights reserved
First edition
Published by Chicago Review Press, Incorporated
814 North Franklin Street
Chicago, Illinois 60610
ISBN 1-55652-271-1
Printed in the United States of America
5

Contents

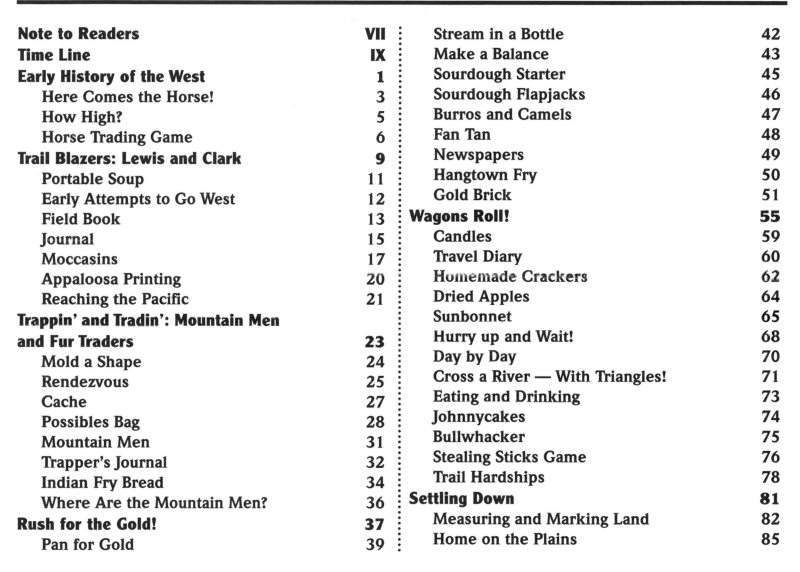

Note to Readers

The terms *Native North Americans* and *North American Indians* are used interchangeably to represent those people who lived in America prior to European settlement. For brevity, when it is clear that the text is referring to one or more Native North American tribes, the term *Indians* is used to refer to all these people.

Time Line

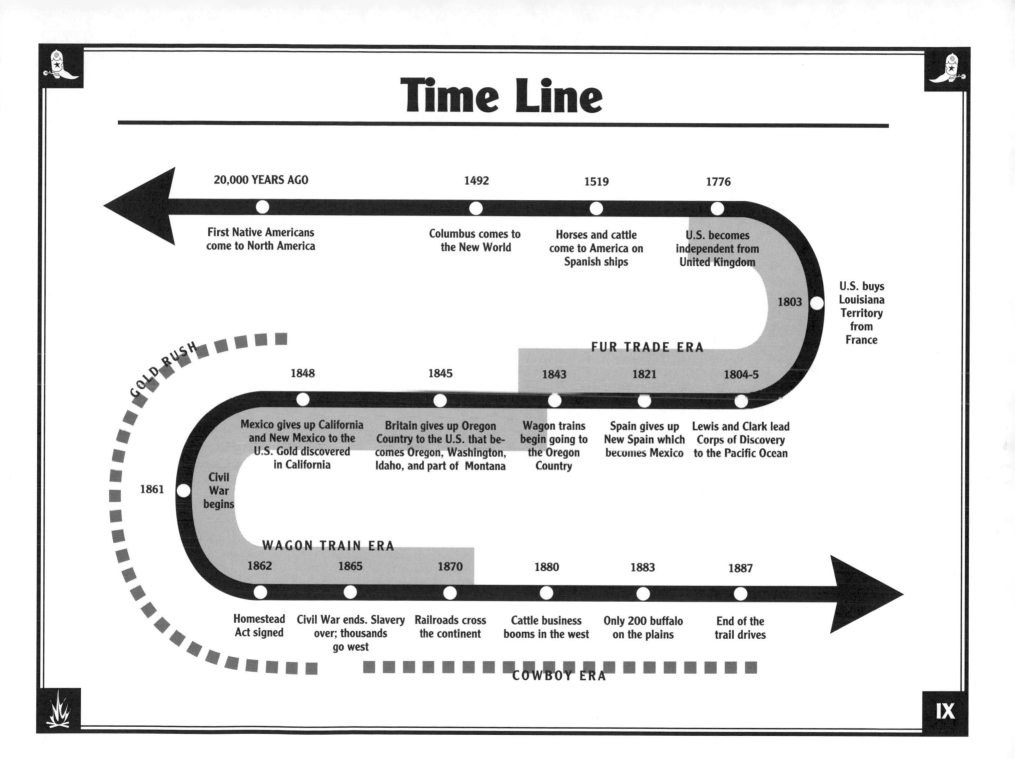

20,000 YEARS AGO

First Native Americans come to North America

1492

Columbus comes to the New World

1519

Horses and cattle come to America on Spanish ships

1776

U.S. becomes independent from United Kingdom

1803

U.S. buys Louisiana Territory from France

FUR TRADE ERA

1848

Mexico gives up California and New Mexico to the U.S. Gold discovered in California

1845

Britain gives up Oregon Country to the U.S. that becomes Oregon, Washington, Idaho, and part of Montana

1843

Wagon trains begin going to the Oregon Country

1821

Spain gives up New Spain which becomes Mexico

1804-5

Lewis and Clark lead Corps of Discovery to the Pacific Ocean

GOLD RUSH

1861

Civil War begins

WAGON TRAIN ERA

1862

Homestead Act signed

1865

Civil War ends. Slavery over; thousands go west

1870

Railroads cross the continent

1880

Cattle business booms in the west

1883

Only 200 buffalo on the plains

1887

End of the trail drives

COWBOY ERA

EARLY HISTORY OF THE WEST

What would you do if your parents told you that your family was going to leave your home behind and walk 2,000 miles through searing deserts and over mile–high mountains? That they were only taking food, blankets, and a few changes of clothing? That the trip would take almost a year? That vicious wild animals and blizzards, poisoned water, and starvation would all be possible? What if they added that they *didn't even have a map* to where you would be going? Whew! Now you know how someone like you might have felt in the 1800s, when people began heading into the American West.

Two hundred years ago most people thought the West was as far away as the moon. Only a few had been to the West and their tales of vast deserts, empty plains, soaring mountains, and hot water geysers seemed unbelievable. People said the land was worthless, the North American Indians were fierce, and grizzly bears were everywhere. Few people thought it would be an interesting place to visit, let alone a place to live. And few could go even if they wanted.

The western part of North America belonged to foreign countries. Spain owned what is now most of Texas and New Mexico, half of Colorado, all of Arizona, Utah, Nevada, and California. Britain controlled the Oregon Country—now Oregon, Washington, Idaho, and part of Montana. Russia owned Alaska; and Hawaii was an independent nation, called the Sandwich Islands. To travel to any of these territories required a passport and special permission of the U.S. and territorial governments.

Maybe the state where you live was once part of a foreign empire. If history had gone differently, you might be speaking a very different language today!

There were native people already living in the West, and when the first settlers came to their lands they were welcomed. North American Indians looked forward to trading goods, selling horses, and learning new things from the newcomers. But so many people moved into the West so quickly that the Indians' lives were changed forever. The settlers took up the land and farmed or fenced it. They killed the buffalo and wild animals for food or skins. The Indians became angry and unhappy. They moved farther west, too, to get away from the masses of newcomers. Tribes fought with each other over land, as the Sioux left Minnesota and the Blackfeet, who had

been called Algonquian, moved from the East. Everyone fought over the land, but that didn't stop them from going west.

Americans went to the West looking for things they couldn't find in the growing cities of the East, like land, fresh air, and clean water. They hated working long hours in factories for only a dollar or two a week. Many people fled starvation or lives of servitude in Europe to settle in the West. After the Civil War many people left the South, including many freed slaves. People wanted to own land of their own, hoped to get rich, or just looked for adventure.

A few people found that the West wasn't what they had expected and went back, but most stayed, and built towns and villages, schools and churches, and tried to make it as much like the place they had left as they could.

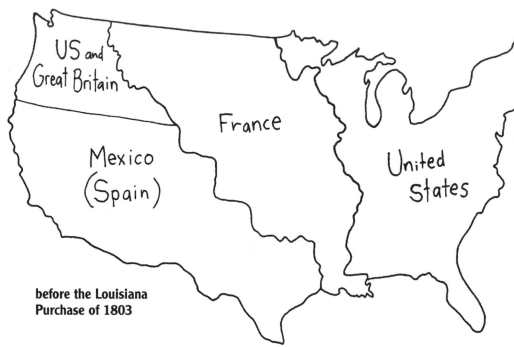

US and Great Britain

France

Mexico (Spain)

United States

before the Louisiana Purchase of 1803

Here Comes the Horse!

Things were very different in western North America long ago. Native North Americans had lived on the plains and deserts of the West for 20,000 years. They lived on the land, planting small gardens, and hunting, fishing, or gathering what they needed. They traveled to trade with others who did the same thing. Then one day, a strange animal arrived that changed their lives forever—the horse.

In 1519, eleven stallions and five mares came ashore from a Spanish ship off the coast of what is now Mexico. Before that arrival, no horses had lived in North or South America since prehistoric times, when a small horse called *eohippus* roamed among the dinosaurs.

Each year the Spanish herds in the New World grew, and horses spread out across the continent. Some

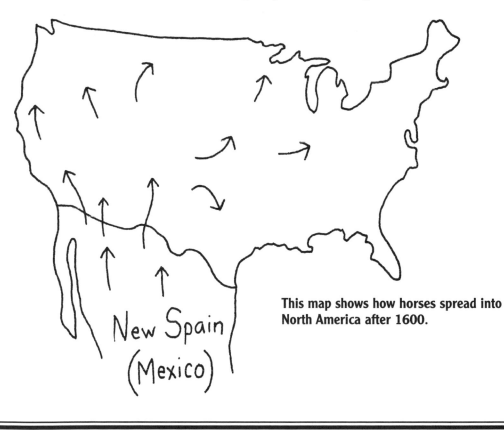

New Spain
(Mexico)

This map shows how horses spread into North America after 1600.

were sold, others stolen. Some escaped the herds and ran wild. When the Native North Americans first saw horses, they couldn't believe their eyes. They had never seen an animal like it before. They had to think of a name for the strange-looking creature. At first they called them god dogs or elk dogs. Some wanted to butcher and eat the animal; others were afraid of it. It wasn't long though before the Indians tamed the horses they caught and learned to ride swiftly across the vast plains. Indians made ropes of grass, hair, or buckskin. They rode without saddles, guiding the horse with the pressure of their knees and by speaking softly to it.

The arrival of the horse was exciting and important. It changed the way the Native North Americans lived in many ways. Before the horses arrived, the Cheyenne, Arapaho, and Dakota Sioux had been farming in small villages. After the Indians acquired horses, they began hunting the huge buffalo herds and traveling in tepee camps across the plains.

With horses, North American tribes could move swiftly and easily. They began to travel farther, raiding other tribes and stealing horses from them. This caused war, something that hadn't been as common before the horse arrived. Men became warriors, not hunters and farmers. Women worked harder than ever, tanning the hides and preserving all the food that buffalo hunters, mounted on horses rather than on foot, now brought to camp.

Soon many tribes had hundreds of horses, people began to count their wealth in horses, and warriors became more important. The simple life of the farm villages had changed forever.

How High?

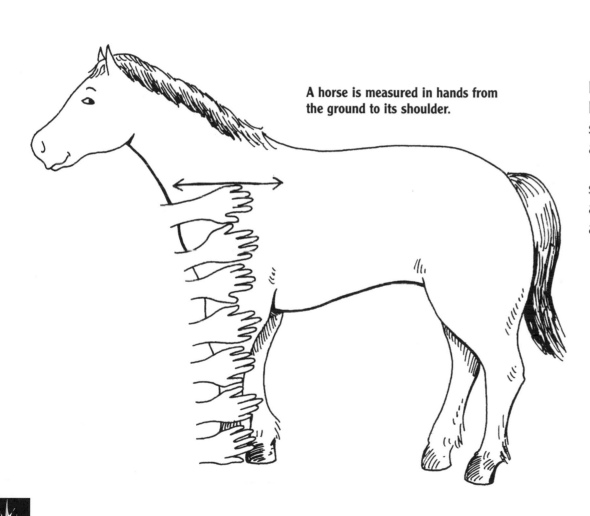

A horse is measured in hands from the ground to its shoulder.

North American Indian horses were small, standing about 14 hands tall. A horse is measured in hands, a hand being 4 inches. To measure a horse you start at the ground, and go up to the shoulder.

How many hands tall are you? Have someone mark your height in inches on a wall with a pencil, then measure it and divide by 4.

Horse Trading Game

Make up a simple card game to help learn the different colors and names of horse breeds.

Draw a horse on the cards.

Materials

Index cards, cut to playing card size

Crayons, markers, and pens

Scissors

Books and magazines with colored photographs of horses

Trace the outline of a horse, like the one shown here. Cut it out and use it as a template or pattern. Trace around the template to make a horse outline on half of the cards. Color in the horse outlines to match the natural colors of horses. (See the list on the following page for assistance.) Write the name of the breed of horse on a separate card. When you are finished, you should have a stack of cards with horses colored on them, and a matching stack of cards with names of the horse markings.

To play, 2 players shuffle the cards, then deal out an uneven number (3 or 5) to each player. Put the rest of the cards in a stack face down on the table. Look over the cards in your hand. If you have a picture of a horse and a breed name that match, this makes a pair. These pairs can be put in a pile beside you. If you make a pair, select the next 2 cards on the stack and add them to your hand. If you can't make a pair, ask the other player for a card you need to make a pair. If she has the card, she gives it to you, and takes another from the top of the stack. If she doesn't have it, you must draw 1 card from the top of the stack, and put a card you don't want at the bottom of the stack. Then it's her turn. Continue playing, making pairs, and discarding cards until the cards are gone. Count up the cards you have in your pairs stack, and see who ends up with the most horses.

Horse Colors and Markings

albino white with blue eyes

Appaloosa spotted rump

bay reddish brown with black mane and tail

buckskin beige with black mane and tail

chestnut bronze or coppery

dappled spotted all over

dun beige with beige mane and tail

grulla bluish-gray

paint white and colored (brown or reddish) areas

palomino light tan or golden with ivory mane and tail

piebald black and white

pinto colors in large patches

roan bay, chestnut, or sorrel sprinkled with gray or white

sabino light red or roan with a white belly

skewbald patches of white over any color except black

sorrel chestnut or brown

Match the types of horses and their names.

TRAIL BLAZERS: LEWIS AND CLARK

In 1803, President Jefferson boldly offered to buy the city of New Orleans from France. Napoleon, Emperor of France, offered to sell him all of Louisiana instead! To pay war debts in Europe, Napoleon sold a huge chunk of land known as Louisiana to the United States for fifteen million dollars. Considering that, at the time, Louisiana included all or part of present day Montana, North Dakota, South Dakota, Wyoming, Minnesota, Nebraska, Iowa, Colorado, Kansas, Missouri, Oklahoma, Texas, New Mexico, Arkansas, and Louisiana, this was quite a bargain. With a stroke of the pen, the United States doubled in size with the Louisiana Purchase!

President Jefferson was excited about the Louisiana Purchase, and immediately sent a group of explorers to check out what America had bought. Young Captain Meriwether Lewis was chosen to lead a Corps of Discovery to inspect the land. He selected Lieutenant William Clark to go with him. Together, they quickly began training a small group of men to travel into the western regions. The party was comprised of thirty men, a North American Indian interpreter, Clark's black slave, and Lewis's dog Scannon.

The Corps set out on foot wearing boots that were soon worn through and so the explorers replaced them with double-soled moccasins traded from the North American Indians. They walked, traded horses with the Indians along the way, or rode small boats on the trip. The explorers took a large supply of gifts for the Indians they were certain to meet along the way. These gifts included beads, shirts, handkerchiefs, mirrors, bells, needles, thimbles, ribbons, kettles, and brass curtain rings that the Indians could wear on their fingers. They also took peace medals with the image of President Jefferson on one side and two hands clasped in friendship on the back.

Equipment they took along included a microscope, a collapsible canoe Lewis had invented, and *portable soup*. Portable soup was made by drying thick broth into a brick which could be carried while traveling. With some water and a few vegetables or roots, the mixture made a healthy hot meal.

Lewis and Clark left Pittsburgh, stopped at St. Louis, Fort Mandan, and made camp on the Pacific Coast which they called Fort Clatsop.

Portable Soup

Bouillon cubes are made from dried broth, much like Captain Lewis's portable soup.

Ingredients

6 bouillon cubes, beef or chicken

3 cups water

2 cans or 1 package frozen mixed vegetables

Utensils

Saucepan

Spoon

(Adult help suggested.)
Heat the water. Add the bouillon cubes, stirring until the cubes dissolve. Stir in the vegetables and heat a few minutes if using canned vegetables. If using frozen vegetables, let the soup simmer following the package directions for cooking the vegetables. Enjoy with crackers!

Early Attempts to Go West

Lewis and Clark were not the first Easterners to try reaching the Pacific Ocean over land. Before Thomas Jefferson became president, he sent an adventurer named John Ledyard on a wild trek across Europe and Asia in a plan to walk overland, cross the Bering Sea in the arctic, and then come east from the Pacific, finally floating by boat down the Missouri River to St. Louis. Ledyard's secret trip was stopped by Catherine the Great, ruler of Russia. When her troops discovered him, he had already walked three thousand miles across Siberia. They escorted him back to Poland.

Jefferson then hired another man to explore the western part of North America, but when he was discovered to be a spy for the French, the expedition was quickly stopped.

When Lewis and Clark and their Corps of Discovery set out, no one knew how far it was to the Pacific Ocean. There were stories of unusual creatures living in the unknown region. Some said there were tribes of man-hating, arrow-shooting, giant women. Others told of devils that looked like people, who were only eighteen inches tall. Other reports said there was a mountain made entirely of salt and fields where gold nuggets lay like walnuts. At one time, people thought the area that's now California was a huge island. But nothing frightened the members of the Corps. They were eager to go into the unknown.

The men took along many blank books to use as journals and diaries. They wrote about everything they saw. They drew sketches of plants, animals, and the Native North Americans they encountered. They drew maps of the country as they went through it. They gathered samples of plants and rocks to take back east for study. They were looking at everything, taking the information back to the people of the United States.

Field Book

Captain Lewis's most valuable item on the trip was his field book. It was bound in elk skin and stored in a tin box to keep it dry. He drew sketches of plants and animals he discovered in the West to take back for scientists to study.

Cover a notebook to create your own field book. Use it to sketch outdoors or just to draw in.

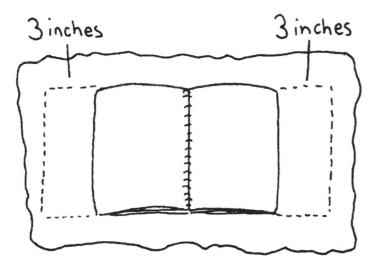

Lay the notebook on the chamois. Trace around it, adding 3 inches at the sides.

Materials

Unlined notebook

Chamois (purchase from auto supply section of supermarket)

Brown embroidery thread or thin yarn

Hand sewing needle with large eye for the yarn

Scissors

Pencil

Colored pens or markers

Spread the chamois flat on a table. Open the notebook and lay it on top of the chamois. Use a pencil to draw a line around the notebook. Then add 3 inches to the right and left sides of the notebook and draw another line. Cut the chamois along this second line. Fold the sides of the chamois

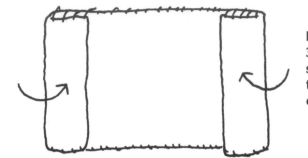

Fold the ends in 3 inches and stitch across the top and bottom edges.

in and stitch the edges of this flap in place by using a stitch called the *blanket stitch*. Continue across the top to stitch down the other side. Knot and clip the thread, tucking the ends inside the cover. Stitch the same way across the bottom. Slip the covers of the notebook inside the chamois cover. If you want to decorate this book cover, use colored pens or markers. Lewis and Clark wrote with dark brown ink.

blanket stitch

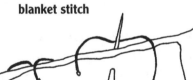

Journal

The Corps kept a set of small journals bound in red goatskin. They were small enough to carry in a pocket. Lewis, Clark, and four other men on the trip took notes about each day's travel, wrote down North American Indian words, and kept track of the weather. They noted phases of the moon, what plants were in bloom, and anything else of interest. They copied each other's notes frequently in case the information was damaged or lost. They stored the journals in tin boxes.

Cover a notebook to use as a journal for yourself.

Trace around the notebook.

Materials
Red construction paper

Small notebook

Pencil

Scissors

White glue

Gold pen

Open the notebook and lay it on top of the red paper. Trace a line around the notebook edges. Then draw another line, about 2 inches from the notebook. Cut along the outer line. Clip the corners and sides to the inner line like the drawing. Fold the edges in around the notebook. Close the notebook and crease the edges securely to shape the cover to fit the notebook. Open and close the notebook a few times to be sure it isn't too tight. Open it again and spread glue along the edges of the notebook that will be covered by the red paper. Smooth it down around the edges of the notebook cover. For a fancy look, use a gold pen to write your name on the cover.

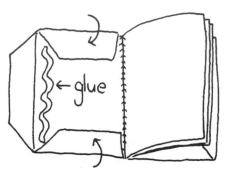

Fold it around the notebook and glue to the cover.

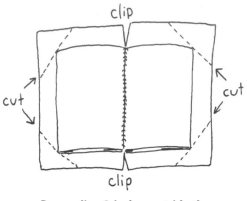

Draw a line 2 inches outside the tracing. Cut on that line.
Cut the corners and clip to the center.

Where are the Lewis and Clark journals today? They are carefully stored at the American Philosophical Society in Philadelphia. The handwritten books are displayed occasionally and at an open house held each October. If your family plans a trip to Philadelphia some October, write for the open house date: American Philosophical Society, 105 S. Fifth Street, Philadelphia, PA 19106-3386. There are also some field notes from the trip kept at the Missouri Historical Society in St. Louis and at Yale University in New Haven, Connecticut.

Sacajawea

A Shoshone girl, about fifteen years old, traveled with the Corps of Discovery. She went with her husband, a French fur trapper Lewis hired to act as an interpreter. The girl's name was Bird Woman or Sacajawea. She had been captured and taken from her people in the Rocky Mountains to live along the Missouri River with another North American Indian tribe. She did a lot of the interpreting once the Corps met with the mountain Indians. She walked or rode in the boats with her baby, Pomp, in a carrier on her back. When the Corps needed to trade with Indians for horses along the way, she did the dealing. Happily, she met her long-lost brother in the mountains. He had become a chief, and helped the Corps with horses and supplies.

Moccasins

It's easy to make yourself a pair of moccasins like the ones that North American Indians made for Lewis and Clark's men. Here's how:

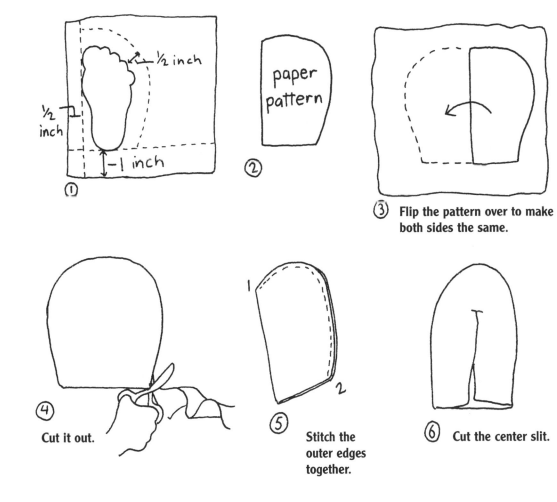

① ½ inch ½ inch 1 inch

② paper pattern

③ Flip the pattern over to make both sides the same.

④ Cut it out.

⑤ Stitch the outer edges together.

⑥ Cut the center slit.

Materials

Typing paper

Pencil

Ruler

Scissors

Chamois (purchase from auto supply section of a supermarket)

Sewing machine, or darning needle and strong thread, or fabric glue

Bright-colored fabric paints

(Adult help suggested.)

First make a pattern from your foot on the typing paper. Measure and draw a line ½-inch from the edge of the paper along the long side of the paper. Measure and draw another line 1 inch from the bottom edge of the paper. Place your foot on the paper so it just touches the lines you've drawn. Draw a curving line ½-inch away from your toes. Draw a straight line along the side of your foot, ½-inch away from your foot.

Cut out the pattern.

Lay the pattern on the chamois and trace around it with a pencil. Flip the paper pattern over and trace around it again, lining up 1 edge like the drawing. This will make a moccasin in 1 piece, with both a top and bottom.

Cut out the moccasin, but don't cut along the center.

Do the sewing on the same side of the moccasin that has lines drawn on it. That way when you are finished and the moccasin is turned right side out, the lines will be hidden inside. Use a sewing machine, set for the longest stitch possible, and stitch the moccasin together along the outside edge, from number 1 to number 2 as shown in the drawing. If using a hand needle or fabric glue, do the same.

Turn the moccasin right side out, and slide your foot into it. Use scissors to cut the top opening, cutting right down the center of the moccasin. Don't cut too far into the toe section. Take your foot out, and cut a 1-inch slit on each side of the center slit.

In the back of the moccasin's bottom section, cut out a rectangle ½-inch from the edge, and 1¼-inches wide. With your pencil, mark an X on each side of this rectangle. Bring the Xs together and stitch on the inside, up the center back of the moccasin. Stitch the bottom closed. You may have to trim or adjust the fit of the moccasin.

Cut a 2-by-3-inch tongue piece for the moccasin. Place the 2-inch-wide edge inside the moccasin along the two 1-inch slits you made on both sides of the

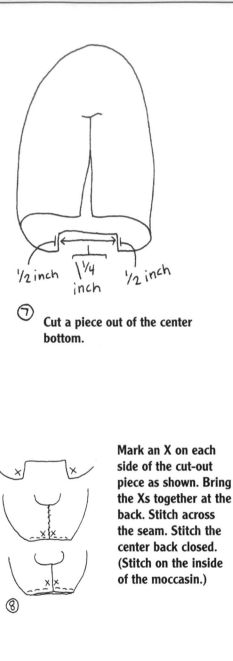

⑦ **Cut a piece out of the center bottom.**

Mark an X on each side of the cut-out piece as shown. Bring the Xs together at the back. Stitch across the seam. Stitch the center back closed. (Stitch on the inside of the moccasin.)

⑧

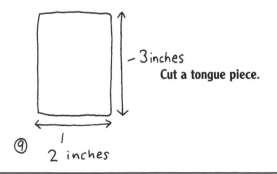

Cut a tongue piece.

⑨ 2 inches

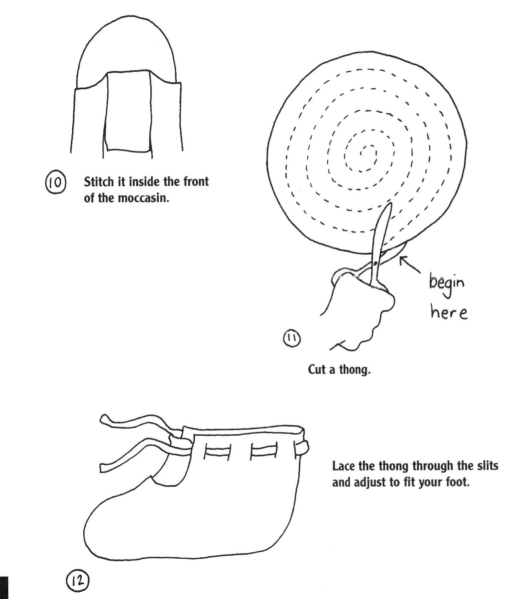

⑩ **Stitch it inside the front of the moccasin.**

⑪ **Cut a thong.**

begin here

Lace the thong through the slits and adjust to fit your foot.

⑫

center opening. Stitch or glue it in place.

Use scissors to cut a long piece of thong for lacing the moccasin to your foot. To do this, cut a circle out of the rest of the chamois, about 4 inches across. Begin cutting a spiral along the outer edge, making the thong about 1/4-inch-wide. Keep cutting until you get to the center, which is the end of the thong. Pull the thong to stretch it.

Use scissors to cut slits around the top of the moccasin to thread the thong through. Don't make the holes too large because leather will stretch a bit. Thread the thong through the holes, adjust the fit of the moccasin to your foot, and tie it in front, over the tongue piece.

Now make a moccasin for the *other* foot. Use the same paper pattern, just flip it over and use the back side to make a moccasin just opposite to the first one you made.

If you want to decorate the moccasins, you can use fabric paints in bright colors. Let the paints dry overnight before wearing the moccasins.

Appaloosa Printing

After crossing the Rocky Mountains the Corps ran low on food. They struggled on, butchering and eating their horses when they had to, until they were discovered by Nez Perce (say it: nez purse) Indians. The Indians gave them roots, but the unusual food made the men sick at first. But with the Indians' help they were able to survive.

Lewis and Clark were impressed with the thousands of beautiful horses the Nez Perce Indians owned. The horses had brightly spotted coats in a range of tans, browns, grays, and reddish browns. They were the horses we call Appaloosas (say it: ap-uh-loo-suh). Today's Appaloosas still have beautiful coloring and wildly spotted hindquarters. The beautiful spotted horses were first raised by the Mongols in ancient China. Spaniards traded for them and brought some to the New World on ships. The Nez Perce Indians prized their huge herds of spotted horses.

Materials

Ink pad with brown or black ink

Colored paper: cream, tan, light gray, or white

You can make some Appaloosa-style notepaper by pressing your thumb or finger into the ink and printing a pattern around the edge of some writing paper. Go ahead and repeat the design around the edges of an envelope to match. Allow both to dry completely before using.

INK

If you want to learn more about these spotted horses, you can visit the museum of the Appaloosa Horse Club, in Idaho, near the spot where Lewis and Clark saw the huge Nez Perce herds. You can see live Appaloosa horses at the museum and horse riding demonstrations in the spring—even Santa Claus on an Appaloosa horse in December! Write to them at: Appaloosa Horse Club, 5010 Highway 8, Moscow, ID 83843.

Reaching the Pacific

When the Corps finally reached the Pacific Ocean they heard it before they saw it. Clark wrote this in his journal, before he even saw the ocean, " . . . the roreing or noise made by the waves brakeing on the rockey Shores may be heard distictly." (He wasn't much of a speller!) They camped on the beach waiting for a ship to come by, hoping to go back to Boston by ship.

That Christmas was a dreary one for the Corps. They built a fort and finally had a roof on it by Christmas Eve, and moved in. Clark wrote in his diary that their Christmas dinner "consisted of pore Elk, so much spoiled that we eate it thro' necessity, some spoiled pounded fish and a fiew roots."

They waited out the winter, but no ship came for them. When spring arrived they headed back the way they had come. It took them only six months to go back. Of the group that left, only one man died—from illness at the beginning of the trip. Another man decided not to return home, and stayed in the mountains with fur trappers for four more years.

When the Corps of Discovery arrived back home they found that most people thought they were lost or dead. They had been gone from home for two years, four months, and ten days. The explorers were treated like heroes everywhere they went. Everyone was eager to hear about their discoveries. The expedition brought back two hundred unknown plants, notes about one hundred twenty-two new animals, along with animal hides, bird skins, and bones from a forty-five-foot dinosaur. Lewis happily shipped a live prairie dog in a cage to President Jefferson, to surprise him with the unusual creature. On the trip they had met fifty different North American Indian tribes, and invited several head men and chiefs to visit the president in Washington City (now Washington, D.C.), which some later did.

Trappin' and Tradin': Mountain Men and Fur Traders

The next people to make the trip west weren't explorers, but fur trappers. They called themselves "mountain men" and traveled into the rugged mountains along the rivers. They used small flat boats and moved them upstream by rowing with long oars, or poling against the river bottom with long poles. Sometimes they walked along the shore, pulling the boat upstream against the current with long ropes. The waterways became their highways. As they worked their way upstream, they set their iron traps along the waterways to catch the animal they were hunting for: the beaver. They could travel easily upstream and could later bring piles of furs downstream to the market.

French and British fur trappers had been trapping across Canada for years. Now the Americans wanted to get in on the trade. Fur traders had tried to get North American Indians to trap for them, but the Indians wouldn't do it. So groups of Americans went upriver to trap. Several men from the Corps of Discovery became guides to trappers, and they started up the Missouri River in boats. It wasn't long before the mountain streams were all being worked by trappers. The men were hunting beavers because of a wildly popular fashion in Europe and the East. Beaver hats were all the rage, and every man of style wanted one. They sold for up to fifty dollars apiece in New York City. The trappers earned about two hundred dollars a year for their work.

After trapping and skinning, the beaver's hide was stretched to dry on a round of willow. Stretched hides were called *plews*. Each plew was marked with the owner's brand. When dry, the hides were folded and pressed with a weight to make bales of them that could be carried long distances. The bales were shipped to London or New York, where they were made into hats.

Mold a Shape

To make a hat from beaver skin, the soft underfur was stripped off the skin by hand. Then it was soaked in hot water and matted into a felt. This felt was shaped into a high-topped hat over a wooden mold. Beaver hats were in high style for about two hundred years.

Materials

Felt scrap, at least 6 by 6 inches

Water

Liquid fabric starch

Teacup

To see how beaver fur was matted, study a piece of felt. Pull a few of the fibers apart. You can see how they were matted together.

Soak the felt in water, then fabric starch. Shape it over a tea cup and let it dry. Pop it off the cup and it will hold its shape.

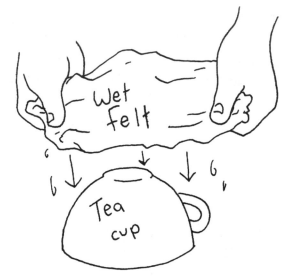

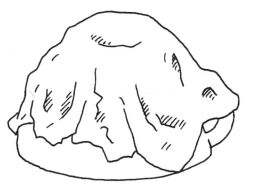

Mold it over the cup to dry.

Rendezvous

The trappers moved along the streams and through the mountains, farther and farther from the fur trading headquarters along the river at St. Louis. Fur companies built trading forts where trappers and North American Indians could bring hides and exchange them for trade goods kept in the fort store. As the trappers captured all of the beavers near the forts and rivers, they had to go farther away, where streams hadn't been trapped yet. This took them into the Rocky Mountains, too far away to make a trip back to get supplies each year. So, the traders began taking the trade goods to the trappers in the mountains. They would load long caravans of mules and pack horses with trade goods and make the trip into the mountains as soon as the snows melted, in order to reach the Rocky Mountains by mid-summer.

When the trading caravan reached the mountains, all the trappers and North American Indians met for a week of trading, visiting, and having fun. Many of the fur trappers were French and they named this trading fair *rendezvous* (say it: ron-day-voo).

Rendezvous took place in the Rocky Mountains each summer. Traders left St. Louis early in spring with caravans of pack mules piled high with bright-colored cloth, beads, kettles, clothing, food, whiskey, traps, and knives. Trappers brought all the beaver hides they had taken during the past winter and spring. Each hide was stretched on a willow branch with rawhide thongs. A stretched beaver hide or plew could be traded in place of money. In fact, there was very little money in the West then. Everything was paid for with plews.

Trade blankets from England had marks woven on the edges, called *points*. The number of points told how many plews were needed to purchase the blanket. Wool blankets were very popular in the Rocky Mountains!

North American Indians also came to the rendezvous. They brought items they had spent the winter making, food they had gathered or prepared, and horses to sell or trade. They were eager to trade for the iron cooking pots, knives, and *foofaraw*. That's what the trappers called ribbons, beads, and other pretty things that Indian women wanted.

Rendezvous was the most exciting time of the year. Not only did people come to trade, they danced to lively tunes played on fiddles or bagpipes, raced horses, held wrestling tournaments, or gambled away their winter's earnings. North American Indian boys from different tribes raced each other, winning horses if they were fast. When it was all over, everyone went back home and the mountain men went back to their trap lines to get ready for the next year.

Fur trading fairs called rendezvous were held at these places in the Rocky Mountains between 1825 and 1850.

Cache

Sometimes travelers and fur traders needed to leave some supplies or baggage behind along the trail. They planned to come back for it later. In order to protect the goods from Native North Americans or other travelers, they put their supplies in a hidden hole in the ground, a *cache* (a French word, say it: cash). A cache was buried secretly, and the extra dirt was piled on a blanket or hide, and taken to a stream where it could wash away. They used other tricks to hide a cache, like digging it in the floor of a tent, then camping over it several days to remove any signs of a hole, or building a camp fire over a buried cache to hide any telltale marks. To find their cache again when they returned, which was sometimes up to a year later, they made a map. On the map they pointed out a nearby marker such as a mound, rock, or tree. They noted the direction and distance to the cache from that point.

Materials
Trowel or shovel

Newspapers

Unopened can of pop or whatever you choose

Paper and pencil

Try caching an unopened can of soda pop for a friend to find. Dig a hole large enough to hold the item you plan to hide. Lay newspapers on the ground and shovel the dirt onto them so no loose dirt is left on the ground to give away the location of the cache. When the hole is large enough, bury the can of pop and cover it up with the same gravel or sod that was removed to make the hole. This will help your hole blend in with the ground around it. Leave no sign of where the cache is buried. Make a map, using a marker such as a tree, fence, rock, or whatever is nearby. Pace off the distance, and mark it on the map. Give the map to a friend, and see if he can find the cache.

Possibles Bag

Mountain men kept flints and dry tinder for starting fires, cloth scraps and other things needed for firing guns, and other valuables in a small skin bag hung from their waist or slung over their shoulder. It was called a *possibles* bag. Inside a possibles bag you might also find a few knives, a letter from a far-off friend, tobacco, a few gold pieces, maybe a small Bible, or anything else a man wanted to take along with him. Here's how to make one for yourself.

Materials

Chamois (purchase from auto supply section of supermarket) or felt

Long leather boot laces

Short, narrow stick

Quick-drying fabric glue

Nail

Pencil

Scissors

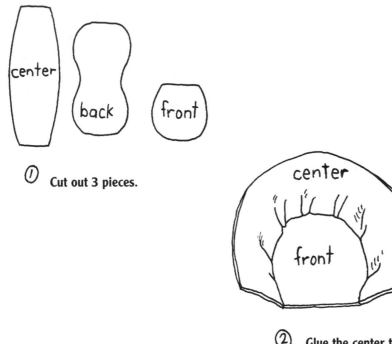

① Cut out 3 pieces.

② Glue the center to the inside of the front section.

Trace the following patterns and cut out a front, a back, and a center piece. Glue 1 long side of the center piece to the front section. Glue a few inches at a time, easing the center piece to fit the curve of the front piece with your fingers. Hold it in place a few seconds to secure it. When that section is completely dry, glue the center piece to the lower back section. Do it the same way, using your fingers to squeeze the pieces to fit. Let dry.

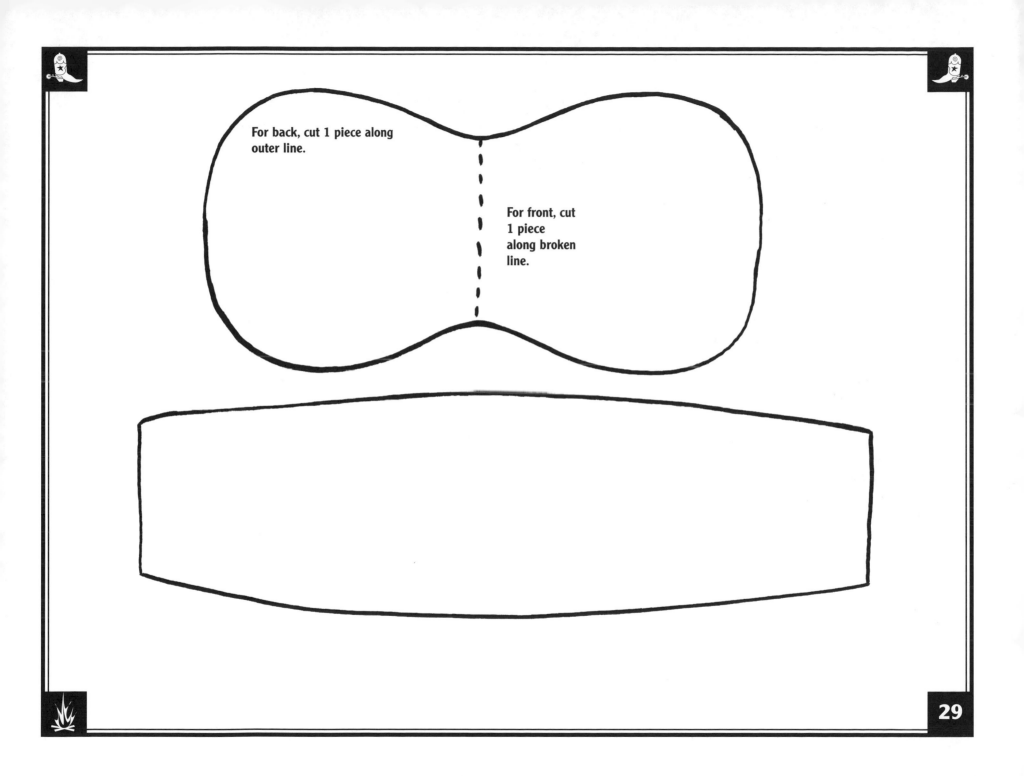

For back, cut 1 piece along outer line.

For front, cut 1 piece along broken line.

Use the point of the nail to poke 2 holes in the back. Thread each end of a boot lace through the holes and knot the ends inside the bag.

Poke 2 holes in the upper center of the front section of the bag. Cut a 3-inch-long piece of boot lacing and push it through the holes, tying the ends in a knot inside the bag.

Cut a piece of boot lacing 8 inches long. Poke a hole in the upper front of the bag, and tie 1 end in a knot through it. Tie a short piece of stick, about 2 inches long, onto the other end of the lacing.

With scissors, cut a hole in the upper front flap of the bag, directly over the loop of lacing. To close the bag's flap, lay this hole over the lacing, pull the lacing up through the hole and slide the end of the stick through the loop. It makes a nifty fastener.

③ Glue the center section to the lower back.

④ Poke 2 holes and tie on a boot lace.

⑤ Fold down the flap. Insert the stick through the loop.

Mountain Men

Mountain men wore simple, durable clothing, and didn't carry much along with them. Their clothes were made from buckskin, and they often wore a hooded coat stitched from a trade blanket. Trousers made from corduroy were favorites, until they wore out. Their heads were covered with warm fur caps and they wore fur-lined moccasins and leggings. If a mountain man couldn't make his own clothing, he traded with North American Indian women who made it. Each man carried a rifle, several skinning knives, and a spyglass. They usually named their rifles, but not their horses. Rifles in those days fired balls of lead or buckshot, and had to be loaded with black gunpowder. If the gunpowder got damp, it wouldn't fire. That could be very risky if an angry grizzly bear was after you. That's where the old saying "keep your powder dry" came from. People sometimes say it now to mean "be careful" or "be prepared."

During their travels, some mountain men rode a horse or mule and took two spare animals to carry supplies and the furs. Others walked, carrying everything on their back in fifty-pound packs. If they didn't have pack animals, they would build a raft or canoe in the spring and float the furs downstream to trade at a fort. In a good season, a man could take almost two hundred plews to trade. Sometimes rough water, unfriendly North American Indians, and pirates made it risky to get the plews to the trading post.

Trapper's Journal

Mountain men got lonely in the wilds, and they looked forward to meeting up with each other and making up tall tales and wild stories over a campfire together. Some of their true stories were nearly unbelievable. Jim Bridger was a famous mountain man. He told this story:

One day I was hunting beaver along the river when a pack of wolves came at me. I was caught a bit unawares, so I ran to the nearest tree and climbed out of reach. Those varmints, they waited around the base of the tree for hours. Then finally they all took off, all but one mean wolf, who stayed on guard. In a half hour or so, the rest of the darned pack came back, and you don't suppose who they had with them? Why, they brought a long-toothed beaver with 'em, to chew down the tree!

Bridger never told how he escaped that one. He and many of the other mountain men were full of interesting stories. Some said Bridger could keep a whole tepee full of North American Indians interested in a wild story for hours, told only with hand signs!

Materials

2 6-by-9-inch pieces of cardboard or tagboard

1 9-by-12-inch piece of brown felt

Several sheets of typing paper

White glue

Scissors

Pencil

Hole punch

Leather bootlace

To make yourself a journal, fold the papers in half to mark the center, then cut the papers down the crease.

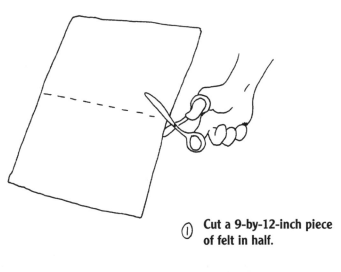

① Cut a 9-by-12-inch piece of felt in half.

6 by 9

② Glue the pieces to the cardboard covers.

Cut the felt in half, so each piece is 6 inches by 9 inches. Glue each piece of cut felt to 1 of the pieces of cardboard to make covers that will be the beaver skin.

Punch holes down the side of 1 cover, then place the other under it, felt side out, and mark spots for matching holes with a pencil. Punch the holes. Mark and punch holes in the papers the same way. When all are prepared, assemble the book, lining up the holes so they match. Thread the bootlace through the holes and tie it in a knot at the end. Trim the ends or, if you like, leave 1 of the ends long and use it as a bookmark or tie a pencil to it.

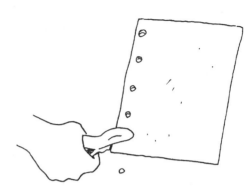

Punch holes in 1 cover. Use it as a pattern to punch holes in the same places on the typing paper and back cover.

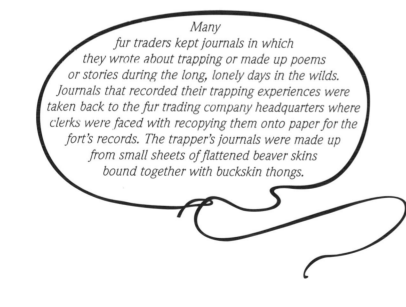

Many fur traders kept journals in which they wrote about trapping or made up poems or stories during the long, lonely days in the wilds. Journals that recorded their trapping experiences were taken back to the fur trading company headquarters where clerks were faced with recopying them onto paper for the fort's records. The trapper's journals were made up from small sheets of flattened beaver skins bound together with buckskin thongs.

Lace a bootlace through the holes and knot the ends.

Indian Fry Bread

Mountain men took only flour, coffee, tea, and salt with them. They found the rest of their food in the mountains. They gathered wild foods like plums and nuts. They hunted deer, antelope, rabbit, and other animals. When times were lean, they ate tree bark, roots, and even their own hide clothing to keep from starving.

Many trappers married North American Indian women and raised families in the mountains. These families helped the trapper with all the work that was needed to prepare the hides. The children worked hard. They worked alongside their parents. Boys tended the *trap line* (a series of traps), skinned beavers, and spent the rest of their time hunting or fishing for the family's food. Girls worked at the same tasks as their mother: cooking, preparing and stretching the hides, tanning deer and elk skins for the family's clothing, and gathering nuts and berries. A trapper's child would have never been able to go to school or play with many other children because they lived so far from other families. Sometimes the family lived with the mother's tribe, which gave the children a chance to see their grandparents and cousins.

If Native North American women had flour, they could make a tasty fried bread. They would have fried it in bear fat or baked it on sticks over a campfire.

Ingredients
Refrigerator biscuits

Cooking oil

Utensils
Frying pan

Tongs or forks

Plate

Paper towels

Topping: powdered sugar, honey, or chili

(Adult help suggested.)

Wash your hands and shape the dough by pulling and pushing the biscuit with your fingers and palms. Make a flat pancake, as thin as you can get it.

Have an adult heat the oil in the frying pan. When it's medium-hot, drop the dough in. Let it cook golden brown, turning once. Drain on a plate covered with paper towels. While it's still warm, drizzle with honey, or sprinkle with powdered sugar. To make a meal, spoon on warm chili.

Press the biscuit as flat as you can before frying.

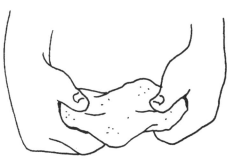

Where Are the Mountain Men?

You might be able to see mountain men today! Members of the American Mountain Man Club hold demonstrations and participate in rendezvous throughout the West during the summer. Members re-create the mountain man part of the past at state parks and schools. They show how trappers made clothing and tools, demonstrate starting a fire by rubbing flint and steel, knife skills, and black powder gun crafting. Their clothing and tools are all handmade, just like they were during the fur trapping era.

You can visit a museum dedicated to the fur trade era: the Museum of the Mountain Man is in Pinedale, Wyoming. It's near the location where rendezvous were held long ago.

What happened to the mountain men? Well, styles and fads change. That's what happened when the China trade was opened up by Captain Cook and his sailing ship. He and other sea captains began bringing ships full of silk from China. Hats made of black silk became the rage. No one wanted to be seen in a beaver hat any more, and so there was no one to sell the furs to. At about the same time, the furs were getting scarce. So many trappers, taking so many animals, had almost wiped out the beaver population. It was the middle of the 1800s, and the end of the fur trade era.

But something surprising had happened in the West that would give more people a reason to make the trip.

RUSH FOR THE GOLD!

One morning in 1848, just after Mexico had given up control of California to the United States, a millwright was checking the equipment at a small sawmill in northern California. He checked the stream coming through the mill yard to make sure it was running clear before the day's work began. That's when he spotted the shiny gold nugget in the water. He and the other sawmill workers kept it a secret because they didn't want people to move in and stop their sawmill business. But it couldn't be kept quiet forever.

People rushed to the area, and when they asked the millwright where to find gold, he pointed to different hills or streams far away, trying to send them off so they wouldn't look near the sawmill. To his surprise, nearly everywhere they prospected they found gold, too. It seemed that the hills of California were nearly full of gold deposits. When the people in the East and Europe heard about it, they flooded to California. They went by wagon train, horseback, and even walking and pushing carts. Boatloads of people left Europe, Mexico, South America, the Sandwich Islands (now called Hawaii), and China. Everyone wanted some of the gold and instant wealth!

The hills became filled with gold seekers in no time, so many prospectors tried looking in other areas of the West. Gold and silver were also found in Nevada, Idaho, Montana, Arizona, New Mexico, Utah, Wyoming, Colorado, and South Dakota. People later went to Canada and Alaska for gold. The first gold seekers to arrive in Nome, Alaska, found gold dust flakes washing up along the beach, coming in with the ocean tide!

The riches weren't found all at once, but it seemed as if they could be anywhere. Whenever someone found a bit of "color," thousands of seekers rushed there to look for more. The biggest gold rush was in California, but for many years there were smaller rushes all over the West.

Towns sprang up almost overnight. Hundreds of people would all head for the mines, but not all of them were miners. Many went to start businesses selling food and supplies to the fortune seekers. They quickly built *muslin towns*, wasting no time felling trees or sawing lumber. The buildings in a muslin town were either tents or houses made with wooden frames and muslin fabric stretched and fastened to the frame. Some towns in the gold rush days had hotels, restaurants, and stores, all made mostly of cloth. Some towns went by the name Ragtown until people stopped searching for gold long enough to decide on a proper name.

Cloth houses and tents couldn't be locked. There were no banks, so everyone kept their gold with them. Miners used to tell an old story about one fellow who, while asleep in his tent, heard a burglar running off with his bag of cash, about six dollars. He jumped off his cot and chased him through town, but didn't catch him. His feet hurt from running over the sharp rocks on the rough street. When he got back home he lit a candle and looked at the bottoms of his feet . . . there were seven dollars worth of gold stuck in the soles of his feet!

There weren't very many women and children in the mining camps at first. Some women decided to open restaurants. Prices for food in mining camps and muslin towns were very high. Women who cooked flapjacks, beans, and coffee for hungry miners, soon made fortunes. One woman did much better than most men in the California mining camps. She baked eighteen thousand dollars worth of pies. She used an iron skillet and a campfire to earn eleven thousand dollars, then bought a cooking stove in which she could bake four pies at a time.

Women's work earned more than men's in mining camps because there were so few women. They cooked or washed clothes—two skills men paid high prices for.

places where gold or silver bonanzas were found

Pan for Gold

People still dream of striking it rich and you can still pan for gold in many places in the West. You can look for *placer* gold easily. That's the kind found in the dirt and gravel of river beds and streams. The gold was washed out of a *lode* (a mass of ore embedded in a rock) into the waterway by erosion.

Gold is heavy, so it sinks to the bottom and gradually sifts down through mud and sand until it rests on rock.

Spring flooding in streams and rivers shifts mud and sand every year, and moves the gold flakes, too. The best time to pan for gold is summer, after the spring runoff has settled the streams.

Most gold nuggets are found along a stream, next to rocks that lie just under the soil or in loose gravel. Look in the slow-moving side of a river or in the curves and bends of a stream.

(Don't be a claim jumper! Be sure you're not trespassing on private land. If you're on public land, look to see if someone has already marked a claim. Look for signs or ask permission first.)

Materials
Pan with sloping sides

Trowel or large spoon

Tweezers

Empty clear plastic pill bottle with lid

Look along a stream bed until you find a large boulder or crevices in a large rock formation. Look for places where gold flakes might have washed and settled. Look along the bank to see how high the spring water line was. Between the high water line and the stream you might find gold that was washed into rock crevices or around a boulder. Dig down in the cracks with either a trowel or large spoon and scoop the material into the gold pan. If there are bits of moss and grass roots, put them in, too. Gold flakes might have washed in between the roots.

Set the pan in a shallow spot along the stream's edge. Let the water wash over the top of the pan. Stir the material with your hand and break the gravel and roots apart over the pan, letting heavy matter sink to the bottom of the pan while the rest washes away in the stream.

Now lift the pan out of the water holding both sides of the pan. Tilt it slowly from side to side, letting some water spill out. Then begin gently swirling the water in the pan around and around. Let more water and dissolved dirt spill out.

During the Gold Rush days, those who went to seek their fortune were called argonauts. Why? The original argonauts were Greeks who searched with Jason for the Golden Fleece, in an ancient Greek myth.

Look for places gold might have settled.

Gold Pans

Use your fingers to search through what remains in the bottom of the pan. Pick out tiny flecks or nuggets with tweezers. Store them in the pill bottle, with a bit of water.

To find gold, miners dug up a handful or two of soil from a rocky stream bank and put it in a gold pan. A gold pan was round, with sloping sides, and small ridges in the bottom of the pan. They worked beside the stream, swirling water mixed with soil in the pan, letting the lighter pieces float out and the heavier ones sink to the bottom of the pan. Gold was heavy, so if there were any particles they would remain stuck in the grooves between the ridges in the bottom of the pan. If a prospector found five to eight tiny flecks of gold, it was a worthwhile spot to work. Then he would get busy, digging and washing out pan after pan, hoping to find larger nuggets.

There's an old story about a lazy miner who would never wash his clothes. Eventually he decided to hang his clothes from a tree branch over a stream, and let the water wash them clean. The next morning, he found them full of gold dust—they were gold plated!

Most miners worked long days, were usually wet and miserable, and were lucky to make ten cents a day. A few miners did find gold chunks that made them rich. The dream of finding the next big chunk was what kept everyone hard at work.

Pick the flecks or nuggets out with tweezers and store them in a pill bottle with a little bit of water.

Stream in a Bottle

It's fun to see how different weights of minerals and soil settle in a stream. You can do it with a bottle.

Materials

2-liter clear plastic soda pop bottle with cap

Spoon

Water

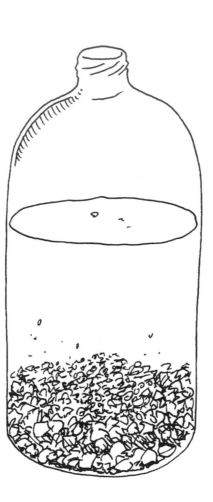

Scoop up or collect different sorts of soil and gravels: some soft clay, some rocky, and other bits of different kinds of soils. Put a few spoonfuls of each type into an empty 2-liter bottle. Add water to fill it ¾ full. Cap it and shake. Watch as the soils settle to the bottom of the bottle. The heaviest goes to the bottom, lighter pieces settle on top. Materials that settle to the bottom in water are called *sediment*.

Scientists think there are ten billion tons of gold in the oceans. Some of it washed there from streams and rivers. A lot of it is in undersea mountains.

Make a Balance

G old and silver were weighed with delicate balances in an *assay office* (where these precious metals were authenticated and weighed) or bank. Here's how to make a simple balance to check the weights of different items.

Pull threads through holes and tie ends together.

Not every gold discovery was for real. Fraudulent people would buy up some gold nuggets or gold dust and scatter it over worthless property. Then they would try to sell the phony gold claim to some unsuspecting miner. This was called salting a claim, *and one clever method they used was shooting at a rocky hillside with a shotgun loaded with gold dust. By the time the unsuspecting buyer discovered there was no other gold on the claim they had purchased, the crook had moved to another location.*

Materials
Empty 2-liter soda pop bottle
Spring-type clothespin
Double-pointed knitting needle or two skewers
2 paper cups
Scissors
Thread
Hole punch or nail
2 Styrofoam packing peanuts

Push the knitting needle or skewers through the center of the clothespin. Make sure both ends extend an equal distance from the clothespin. Insert the tip of the clothespin into the bottle opening.

Cut the paper cups down, so the sides are only about 2 inches high. Punch 3 holes, equal distances apart, in the top of the cup. Cut 6 equal lengths of thread. Pull 1 thread through each hole in each cup and knot it on the outside of the cup. Tie the 3 strings together at the other end.

Do this for the other cup. Slide 1 threaded cup on one end of the knitting needle or skewers; slide the other cup on the opposite end. Push a Styrofoam peanut onto the ends of the needle or skewers to keep the cups from falling off. Experiment with the weights of different items, seeing how many items such as jelly beans must be placed in 1 cup to equal the weight of a handful of pennies in the other cup, for example. When 2 items are the same weight, the skewer will be straight across. If 1 side weighs more, it will sink lower than the other.

To weigh gold, a piece of known weight, such as exactly 1 ounce, would be put on 1 side of a balance, and gold dust added to the other side until both sides were equal.

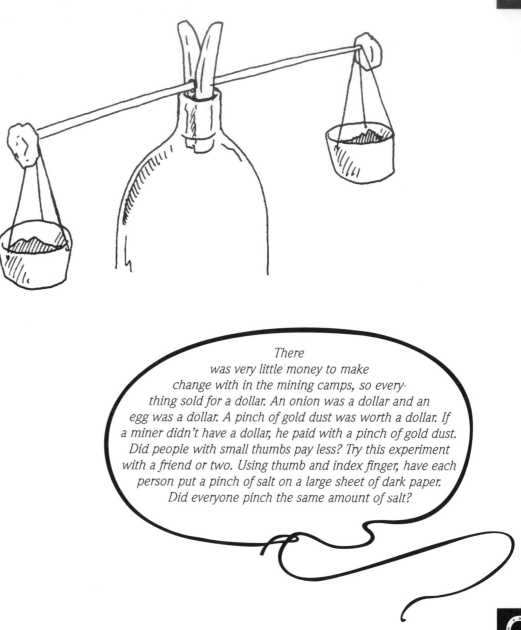

There was very little money to make change with in the mining camps, so everything sold for a dollar. An onion was a dollar and an egg was a dollar. A pinch of gold dust was worth a dollar. If a miner didn't have a dollar, he paid with a pinch of gold dust. Did people with small thumbs pay less? Try this experiment with a friend or two. Using thumb and index finger, have each person put a pinch of salt on a large sheet of dark paper. Did everyone pinch the same amount of salt?

Sourdough Starter

Yeast and other baking supplies were often hard to come by. Miners and cooks used a homemade *sourdough starter* that caused bubbles of air in bread dough, making it rise. Starters were made in many different ways. They were easy to make, and gave baked goods a distinctive taste.

Here are two ways to make the starter for flapjacks. Use either one to make the starter a few days before making the flapjacks.

Starter One

Ingredients
1 package dry yeast
½ cup lukewarm water
2 cups warm water
2 cups flour
1 tablespoon sugar

Utensils
Mixing bowl
Measuring cup
Glass jar
Paper towel
Spoon

Dissolve the yeast in ½ cup lukewarm water. Stir in 2 cups of warm water. Next stir in the flour and then the sugar. Stir until it's smooth. Pour into a jar and cover with a paper towel. Let it sit at room temperature until bubbles form. It may take up to 5 days. Stir the mixture with a spoon 2 or 3 times a day.

Starter Two

Make this one with potato water.

Ingredients
2 medium-sized potatoes, cut into cubes
3 cups water
2 cups flour
1 tablespoon of sugar

Utensils
Saucepan
Spoon
Glass jar
Paper towel

(Adult help suggested.)
First make potato water by boiling the potato cubes in the water for 15 minutes. Remove the potatoes and measure out 2 cups of the remaining liquid.

Mix the 2 cups of potato water with the flour and sugar into a smooth paste. Put it in the jar and cover with a paper towel. Set it in a warm place until the mixture bubbles and doubles in size. It may take 1 or 2 days.

45

Sourdough Flapjacks

For either starter:

Whenever you use some of the starter for a recipe, you need to add more to the remaining starter mixture to keep it going. To replace 1 cup of starter taken out, mix ¾ cup flour with ¾ cup lukewarm water and 1 teaspoon of sugar. Add to the remaining starter. After bubbles form in the starter again, it can be stored in the refrigerator. Every 10 days, add 1 teaspoon of sugar to the starter kept in the refrigerator. The sugar feeds the bacteria, so they keep making bubbles.

Ingredients
1 cup flour

2 tablespoons sugar

1½ teaspoon baking powder

½ teaspoon salt

½ teaspoon baking soda

1 beaten egg

1 cup starter

¾ cup milk

3 tablespoons cooking oil

Molasses or syrup, to taste

Utensils
Measuring cup

Mixing bowl

Mixing spoon

Tablespoon

Pancake turner

Frying pan or griddle

(Adult help suggested.)

Mix the egg, starter, milk, and 2 tablespoons oil in the bowl. Stir until it's smooth. Add the rest of the ingredients. Stir until smooth.

Place 1 tablespoon of oil in a griddle or frying pan and heat it at medium heat.

Use 2 tablespoons of batter for each flapjack. Fry until bubbles appear in the batter of the flapjack. When the bubbles begin to burst, flip it over and fry the other side until it is golden brown. Serves 4.

Miners enjoyed molasses poured over a stack of flapjacks. Syrup goes nicely, too.

Burros and Camels

To get to the mines, the miners led donkeys that carried packs on their backs. These donkeys, which they called *burros*, were lively animals and they often ate the miners' flour, sugar, bacon—anything they could find in camp to eat. Some ate wool shirts—everything except the pick and shovel! Miners, also called *prospectors*, had to keep an eye on their burros nearly all the time.

Here's an old joke about prospectors and burros:

The newcomer asked the old miner, "How many years have you been a prospector?"

"Thirty years," the old fellow said.

"You prospected for thirty years?" the newcomer asked in surprise.

"No, I prospected for five years," the old fellow said.

"Wait. You said you've been a prospector for thirty years, but you've only prospected for five years. How can that be?" the newcomer asked.

"It's a fact," the miner said. "Five years I prospected and the other twenty-five were spent looking for my burros."

Did you know that camels were once part of the story of the West? The Viceroy of Egypt donated the first herd, which the U.S. Army used to pack supplies in the Southwest. They worked out just fine in that desert region, so more were imported. Since people taking supplies to the mining camps needed pack animals, camel pack trains were loaded with barrels, sacks of food, and tools and marched to the camps. Camels could carry twice as much as a mule, and they found their own food along the way.

However, camels presented some unique problems. Their feet had to be covered with rawhide or canvas boots for rocky or muddy ground. Horses and mules panicked and ran off when they smelled or saw the strange beasts. That created so much trouble along the trails and in the towns that after a few years all the camels were sold or turned loose. But it's true—camel pack trains once roamed the trails of Arizona, Texas, New Mexico, California, Montana, Idaho, and Washington state, as well as British Columbia.

Fan Tan

Many gold seekers came from China. They called California the Land of the Golden Mountain, and were determined to find their fortune in gold and return to China with wealth. The Chinese miners were nearly all men. During the long ship voyage from China they told many stories about how they would find gold nuggets the size of goose eggs.

Many American miners were angry to see so many others trying to find the gold. They made laws to keep immigrants out of the mining areas, or to charge them to look for gold. It became harder for the Chinese to mine for gold. Once a dig site was thoroughly worked over and no one found any more flecks, they would all leave for another promising location. This is when Chinese miners would be allowed to rework this abandoned area. They sometimes found gold the others had missed.

Fan Tan was a popular game of chance played by Chinese miners. Players enjoyed it because everyone has a fifty-fifty chance of winning and it takes no skill to play. They would bet on the outcome: odd or even.

Materials

Dry beans

Large spoon

Use a large spoon for a rake; the Chinese fan tan dealers used rakes with handles made of ivory. You can use beans: they used round coins made of brass which had square holes in the middle.

To play, put a pile of dry beans (a handful or 2 is enough) in the center of a table. The players pick sides: odd or even. The dealer begins the game by raking the beans out of the pile, 2 at a time. When she gets to the last of the pile, the winner is clear: if 1 bean remains, odd wins. If 2 beans remain, even wins. A new, unknown number of beans must be piled on the table each time so that everyone has an equal chance on every turn.

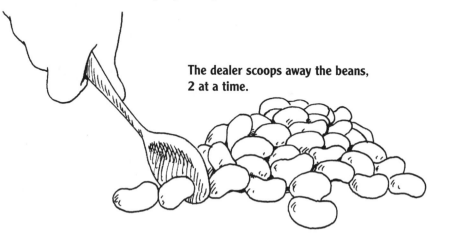

The dealer scoops away the beans, 2 at a time.

odd

even

If 1 bean is left, odd wins.   If a pair is left, even wins.

Newspapers

Many prospectors gave up looking for gold and got other jobs in the growing towns. One was Samuel Clemens, a young man who went to Nevada with plans to mine silver. The town newspaper's editor was impressed with the letters that Samuel wrote to the newspaper, so he offered him a writing job. Samuel quickly accepted, because the twenty-five dollars a week salary was more than he was able to make looking for silver. Samuel later wrote books using the pen name, Mark Twain. Perhaps you've read two of his best-known books: *The Adventures of Tom Sawyer* and *The Adventures of Huckleberry Finn*. What if he'd struck it rich in silver, and never turned to that newspaper job?

Newspapers were important in the mining towns. The law required miners to pay for newspaper advertisements describing their claim. This way other miners would know where the section of land one miner claimed mining rights to was located. Newspaper editors traveled from one muslin town to another with printing presses, to make quick money printing little newspapers that were mostly advertisements.

Newspapers also printed a lot of exciting stories about people finding gold. Then the papers were sent east, so that people would read about the fabulous finds, and hurry out west to the town. When they got there, local merchants would sell them mining claims, supplies, tents, and food. One newspaper in Colorado tried to create excitement about a new gold discovery and hoped to bring newcomers flocking to the town. They printed the first edition of the paper in gold ink—made from real gold!

> Children in the gold camps and muslin towns led either a harsh or a wild life. There was seldom a school or church, and their parents were busy working long hours so the children were left to take care of themselves. By the age of six, boys were out panning in creek beds. Girls worked in laundries, carrying water, and scrubbing clothes. Some children would sweep out the stores every morning with small brooms and dustpans, scraping up any gold dust that had fallen during business the day before. Others became thieves or gamblers. Unless their parents happened to strike it rich, children led harsh lives.

Hangtown Fry

If a lucky miner did strike it rich, the custom was to go to the town restaurant and order the most expensive meal on the menu. Cooks called it Hangtown Fry and it was made from fresh eggs, bacon, and oysters. There wasn't much else to choose from in a mining boomtown.

Ingredients

¹/₂ pound bacon

2 tablespoons cooking oil

1 small can oysters

¹/₄ cup flour

6 eggs

Salt and pepper, to taste

Utensils

Frying pan

Plate

Paper towels

Bowl

Whisk

Spatula

(Adult help suggested.)
Fry the bacon, remove from the frying pan, and let it drain on a plate covered with paper towels.

Drain the liquid from the can of oysters. Roll them in the flour until they are coated. Put the floured oysters in a frying pan with the oil. Fry until crisp, turning them so both sides are golden brown.

Beat the eggs in the bowl. Season them with a dash of salt and pepper. Pour the eggs over the oysters in the frying pan. Cook for a few minutes, then lay the bacon strips over the top of the eggs. Turn and fry the other side golden brown. This will make enough for 4 people.

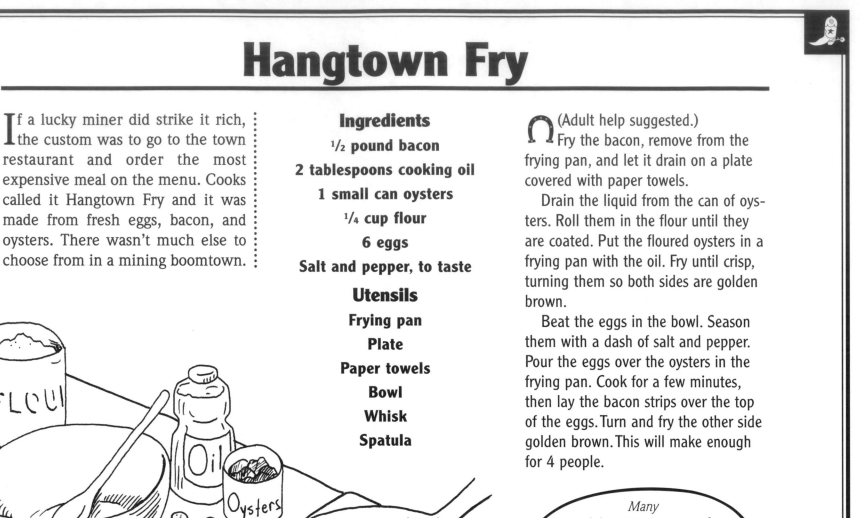

Many mining camps ran out of salt. Some of the miners then sprinkled gunpowder on their food instead. Settlers commonly substituted white wood ashes from the cook stove in place of salt.

Gold Brick

You can get an idea of the amazing weight of gold by making a gold brick from a grocery bag. Make a brick 5 inches high, 5 inches wide, and 6 inches long. If it were solid gold, it would weigh 100 pounds!

Materials

Large paper grocery bag, or large piece of paper

Ruler

Pencil

Scissors

Glue

Measure out 2 patterns: 1 will be a square, 5 inches long on all 4 sides. The other will be a rectangle; 2 sides will be 5 inches long, the other 2 sides will be 6 inches long. Cut out both to use as tracing patterns.

Follow the diagram to lay out the patterns, tracing around each. Add 1-inch flaps where indicated for folding and gluing the box together.

Cut out the diagram and fold along the lines to make a box shape. Spread glue on the flaps and fold them inside the box, holding it carefully until it is secure.

Use the patterns to draw this shape. Draw 1-inch-wide flaps on the sides like this. Cut, fold, and paste to make a gold brick.

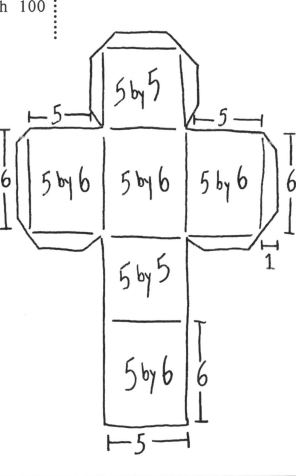

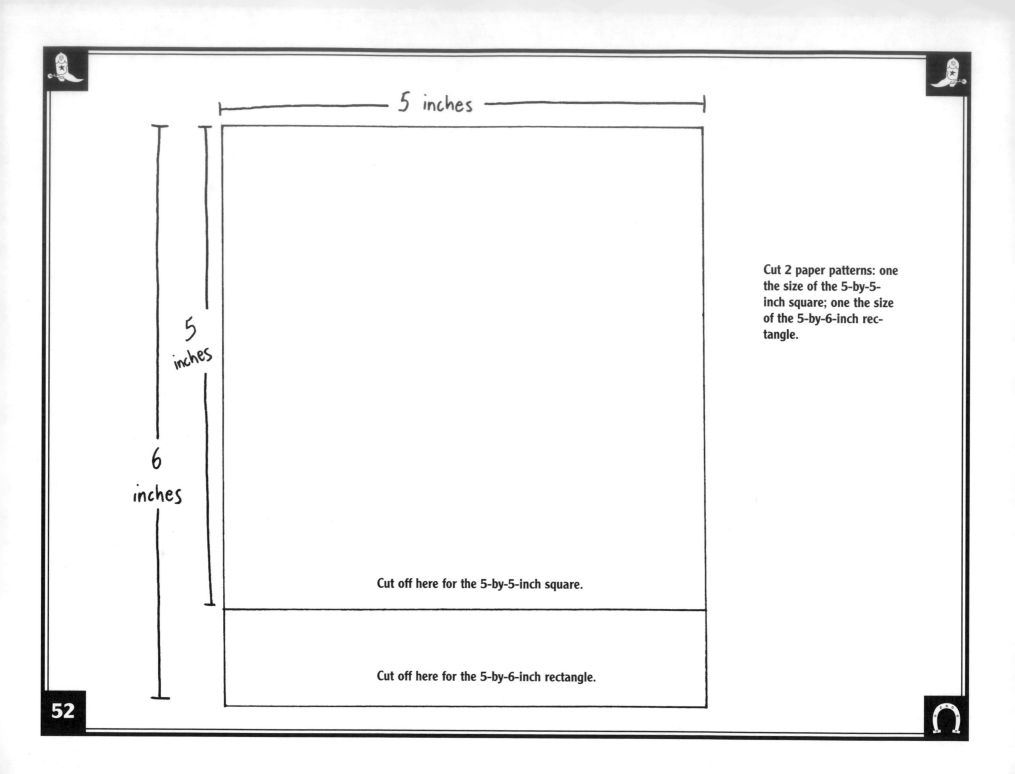

5 inches

5 inches

6 inches

Cut 2 paper patterns: one the size of the 5-by-5-inch square; one the size of the 5-by-6-inch rectangle.

Cut off here for the 5-by-5-inch square.

Cut off here for the 5-by-6-inch rectangle.

During the California Gold Rush, gold was worth $15 an ounce. How much was a brick this size worth then?

1. Multiply 100 (the number of pounds in the brick) by 16 (the number of ounces in one pound).
2. 100 x 16 = 1,600 or 1,600 ounces.
3. Multiply 1,600 ounces by $15 (the price per ounce).
   1,600 x $15 = $24,000

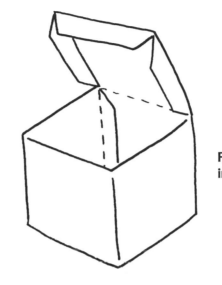

Fold and glue the flaps inside the box.

You'll discover that a brick of gold like the one you made was worth twenty-four thousand dollars in old California. That was a lot of money in those days, when people earned only two or three dollars a week from factory jobs!

How much would a gold brick like the one you just made be worth today? Check the newspaper for today's gold price. The price is listed on the stock market report page of the newspaper, usually under a heading called Metals Market or something similar. When this was written, gold was $380 an ounce. That means that your brick would be worth $608,000!

WAGONS ROLL!

News of California gold arrived in the East in the winter of 1848. By spring there were thousands of people waiting at the *jumping-off towns* along the Missouri River. Independence, Missouri, and Westport Landing, now a part of Kansas City, were important towns where travelers readied their wagons for the trip.

People had been traveling to Oregon Territory in wagon trains for a few years before the California gold rush began. They wrote letters back to friends and relatives in the East, telling them about the climate and the good farmland in Oregon and urging them to come. Letters had to be taken east by ship, around the tip of South America, and then to Boston. It took two or three years to receive a reply from a letter sent this way. When letters from Oregon arrived in the East, they were read aloud at church services and community meetings. People listened with interest. Could things be better so far away? It was something nearly everyone in the East thought about.

More people began outfitting themselves to make the trip to Oregon, and the number of wagons crossing to the West grew each year. The real rush began when word got out about the newly discovered gold in California. When people heard about the free gold and silver, the land that could be farmed, and the excitement out West, thousands joined up in wagon trains. People sold everything, borrowed money, and headed for California. Years before, people had thought California was an island—it was drawn that way on early Spanish maps. Now they knew it could be reached by traveling overland across the Plains, crossing the Great Desert, then passing over the mountains called the Sierra Nevadas.

Most families that went West in wagon trains traveled with other relatives who were going, too. Sometimes neighbors decided to sell their farms in the East and go together. They planned to settle next to each other in a new place. Some groups went together because they belonged to the same church. Hundreds of different groups organized; one was all

French, one all German, one all Methodist, another all Harvard College graduates. One wagon train was all Cherokee Indians, and another was led by the matron of Sing Sing Prison and had three widows and fifteen men in the group. Even a few small towns picked up and moved west together. People were in a frenzy, talking of nothing except going west.

Meetings were held to discuss whether or not to make the trip. Newspapers printed letters and stories about what it was like in Oregon and California—stories which were often made up by writers who had never been there! Letters and gossip fueled the dreams of those who wondered what the trip would be like.

Once a family decided to go, they sold almost everything they owned. It was necessary to save up quite a bit of money in order to purchase a proper wagon, teams of oxen, and supplies for a year. It took about one thousand dollars to make the trip, at a time when people earned only a few dollars a week. Most poor people were unable to make the trip. Many families were able to borrow money from relatives. Some people were able to hire on with other families as servants, working for them in exchange for passage.

A family making the trip planned to spend several months on the trail. Here's a list of basic supplies they were advised to take:

1,000 pounds of flour (that's 100 ten-pound sacks today)

600 pounds of bacon or pork (that would be 600 packages as sold in today's stores)

150 pounds of sugar

Saleratus, or yeast powders, for making bread

50 pounds of lard (that would be 25 cans of shortening today)

½ bushel of dry beans (that's about 8 gallons—8 filled milk jugs from today's stores)

75 pounds of rice

100 pounds of coffee (that's 50 two-pound cans today)

10-gallon wooden barrel of water, to refill along the way

Matches

Candles

Soap

Spare shoes for the oxen or horses

Year's supply of woolen trousers for men and boys

Extra shoes for everybody

2 wool blankets for each person

First aid supplies: usually herbs and bandages

Plows, tools, and equipment for building and farming

Money

People expected to hunt along the way for fresh meat, but they needed to take money to buy extra supplies along the way. Fur trade forts sold food items to travelers, and Native North Americans sold them vegetables from their gardens. Money was also needed to pay for building supplies, seed for the first crop, and food for the family's first winter in the new land.

The Oregon Trail went to Oregon City.
If you turned toward California, you could go through
Salt Lake City or bypass it. Many people and animals
died looking for shortcuts and cutoffs along the way.

It was important that a family take enough supplies for the length of the trip, but not too much so that the oxen would be overburdened.

Wagons for the trip were specially built for those who could afford them. Conestogas were large heavy wagons built by German craftsmen in Pennsylvania. Big Conestoga wagons hauled the first wave of settlers over the Appalachian Mountains, but the heavy wagons proved too heavy for the distance and mountains of the Oregon Trail. Emigrants who took them found out that the expensive handcrafted wagons were too big for their animals to pull. For the trip west, smaller farm wagons were easiest on the animals, and most likely to get all the way through to their destination.

Women wove new white canvas for wagon covers. It was tied on over the hoops to create a roof for the wagon that provided shelter from rain and shade from the sun. The sides of the covering could be adjusted and were usually rolled up so breezes could blow through, cooling off the wagon's interior. The wagons had high wheels so the axle would clear rocks and tree stumps. The body had sloping ends so the cargo settled in the middle and wouldn't slide out going up or downhill.

Women spun the stems of flax plants and wove it into linen fabric to cover the wagons. They also wove heavy fabric for sacks to pack supplies in. All the seams had to be sewn by hand—the sewing machine hadn't been invented yet. The wagon boxes were often painted a bright blue, the wheels red, and shining white cloth stretched over the bent hickory bows. The rows of red-, white-, and blue-colored wagons must have been a pretty exciting sight!

The women and girls made *feather ticks* to use as beds. They sewed large fabric sacks, and filled them with chicken and duck feathers. The whole family worked into the night every evening getting things made. They worked by the light of candles that had to be handmade, too.

Candles

Materials

Sheet of honeycomb beeswax (purchase at craft store)

Candlewick (as long as you want the candle to be plus 2 inches)

Paring knife

Scissors

Bath towel

Lay the bath towel on a work table to provide a soft surface to work on.

Use the paring knife to cut the wax to the length you want the candle to be. Lay the wick along the edge of the wax sheet and gently begin rolling it up. Press firmly and evenly as you roll, until the whole sheet is rolled up around the wick. Trim the wick so it's about ½ inch above the wax.

Measure out the size of a wagon bed, and imagine packing your family and supplies in that much space. Conestoga wagon beds were sixteen feet long and four feet wide. (Farm wagons were smaller.) Make a list of the things you would take along if you were making the trip. What would you leave behind? It must have been difficult for people to decide what to take and hard to part with favorite toys, books, and pets.

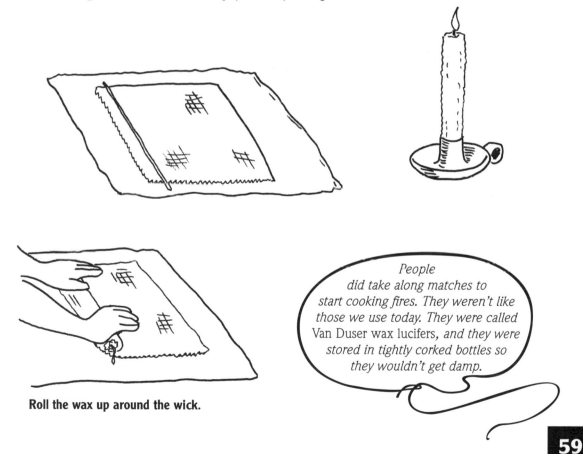

Roll the wax up around the wick.

People did take along matches to start cooking fires. They weren't like those we use today. They were called Van Duser wax lucifers, *and they were stored in tightly corked bottles so they wouldn't get damp.*

Travel Diary

Before leaving home, many families were given going-away parties. Friends brought gifts for the trip: clothing, flower seeds to tuck in the baggage somewhere, and food to eat during the first few days of travel. Many people were given diaries so they could record the great adventure. Here's how to make one of your own.

Stitch blank paper together on top of the endpaper.

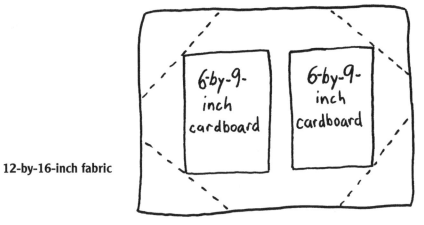

12-by-16-inch fabric

Materials

8 sheets of typing paper (8½ by 11 inches)

1 sheet colored paper, wallpaper, or gift wrap (8½ by 11 inches)

2 6-by-9-inch cardboard pieces

1 piece of woven fabric (12 by 16 inches)

Scissors

Glue

Darning needle and heavy thread or long-armed stapler

Lay 8 pieces of paper in a stack. Place the gift wrap or other fancy paper at the bottom of the stack, with the pretty side facing the white papers. This piece is the endpaper. Sew or staple through the center of all the pages. (You can also use a sewing machine. If you do, set the stitch length to make the longest stitch possible and sew slowly.)

If you are stitching by hand, poke the needle through the papers and stitch as shown in the drawing. Don't pull the thread too tightly. Knot the thread when you are finished, and trim the end. Set the pages aside.

Lay the fabric with the wrong side facing up. Center the cardboard pieces on it leaving a ½-inch space between them. Trim the corners of the fabric away. This will help the corners lie flat when the fabric is glued down.

Spread glue on the edges of the cardboard and fold the fabric over it. Press down neatly.

Spread glue over the rest of the cover where the cardboard is showing, except on the fabric lying between the cardboard pieces. This part in the middle will become your book's "spine."

Lay the pages on top of the glued cardboard, pressing the back of the endpapers into the glue. Next, open and close the book several times to adjust the cover smoothly. Wipe away any extra glue so that the pages won't stick to the cover.

After it dries, it's ready for you to fill with your thoughts and feelings and the things you see and do each day. Don't worry that it won't seem exciting—most diaries tell of the small and ordinary things that happen each day. When people read a diary years later they are able to see how people lived and felt at the time.

A Girl's Diary

Here's what a girl named Sallie wrote in her diary while her family waited at the jumping-off town of St. Joseph, Missouri, in the spring of 1849:

We expect to remain here several days, laying in supplies for the trip and waiting our turn to be ferried across the river. As far as eye can reach, so great is the emigration, you see nothing but wagons. This town presents a striking appearance—a vast army on wheels—crowds of men, women, and lots of children and last but not least the cattle and horses upon which our lives depend.

Some people wrote diaries that they intended to send back to friends or to newspapers to be published. They thought that the information would help people who made the trip later.

Fold and glue fabric to the cardboard pieces.

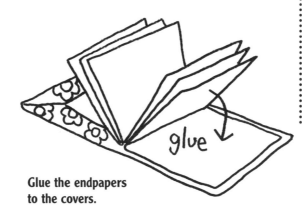

Glue the endpapers to the covers.

Homemade Crackers

Before they left their homes, women and children baked flour into breads, doughnuts, and crackers they could take along for meals. They packed them in tins to keep them from getting damp or moldy. Here's a recipe to make homemade crackers.

Ingredients

1 cup flour

1 teaspoon baking powder

Pinch of salt

$1/2$ cube butter or margarine

$1/4$ cup milk

Utensils

Mixing bowl

Fork

Spoon for mixing

Measuring cup

Rolling pin

Table knife

Baking sheet, greased with shortening

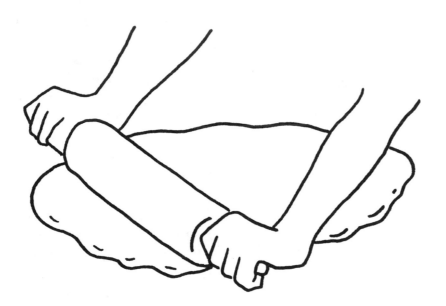

Roll the dough flat.

(Adult help suggested.)

Preheat the oven to 400° F.

Mix the flour, baking powder, and salt in the bowl. Use the fork to mash in the butter until the mixture looks like crumbs. Add the milk and stir until the dough mixture forms into a ball.

Sprinkle flour on the counter and roll the dough flat with a rolling pin. Cover the rolling pin with a dusting of flour to keep the dough from sticking to it. Roll the dough into a rectangle or square shape. Roll it as flat as you can. Use the knife to cut the dough into small square or rectangle crackers. Place the crackers onto the greased baking sheet. Poke with a fork and bake for 9 minutes. This recipe makes about 24 crackers.

Cut into rectangles and poke holes with a fork.

Dried Apples

Dried apples were a staple in every wagon. Long before leaving home, a family made a large supply of dried apples.

People dried apples by slicing them thinly and stringing them across the inside of the house and over the fireplace where it was warm. When the rings were dry, they were packed away and used to make apple pie and apple crisp, or to munch on when there was no time to build a fire and cook a meal.

Ingredients

4 red or green apples

1 cup lemon juice or lemon-lime soft drink

Utensils

Small bowl

Knife

Spoon

String, about 3 feet long

2 thumbtacks

Wash and dry the apples. Slice the apples across, so they are round, like donuts. Use a spoon to carve out the center section with the seeds. Pour the lemon juice into a small bowl. Dip each slice into the lemon juice. The acid in the lemon juice will keep the apple from turning brown. After the slices have been dipped, thread the string through the center of the slices and hang it up with thumbtacks to dry. Drying time depends on thickness of the slices, climate, and room temperature.

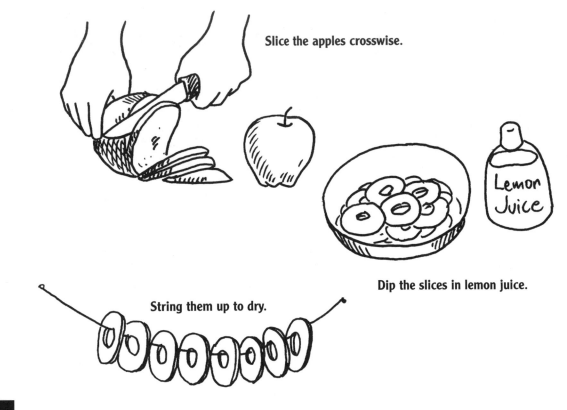

Slice the apples crosswise.

Dip the slices in lemon juice.

String them up to dry.

Sunbonnet

In the 1800s women and girls always wore hats. City women preferred fashionable hats woven from straw with lavish ribbons or flower decorations. Most farm women wore sunbonnets they made themselves. Women and girls in the wagon trains nearly all wore big sunbonnets to keep the sun and dust off their faces. The wide brim and long back cape protected their skin against tanning, sunburn, and freckles—all very unfashionable in those days. They sewed their bonnets by hand and made them from gingham or seersucker, usually in brown, gray, or black. Those colors were easier to keep clean on the dusty trip. Rarely were bonnets made in bright colors—even for girls. It just wasn't considered proper.

Sunbonnets had sections in the brim where *slats* could be slipped in. Slats were strips of pasteboard (like cardboard). The slats kept the brim stiff, and could be slipped out for washing.

Here's how to make a sunbonnet for yourself, or someone else. It's just the thing for a sunny day at the beach or to wear while gardening.

Materials

Newspaper

Pencil

Scissors

Straight pins

½ yard of cotton cloth

Ruler

Thread

Hand sewing needle

Steam iron

Sewing machine

3 yards of 1-inch wide ribbon

Follow the diagrams to draw a pattern for your bonnet on a sheet of newspaper. Cut out the pattern. Pin the patterns to the fabric and cut them out. Be sure you have cut out 2 brims and 1 bonnet piece.

Pin the 2 brim pieces together, with the right sides of the fabric facing each other, the wrong sides out. Stitch along the curved edge of the brims. Make the seam ⅝-inch-wide.

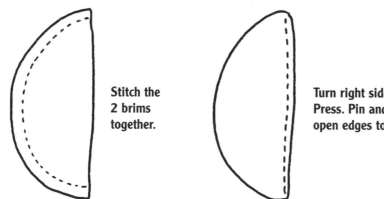

Stitch the 2 brims together.

Turn right side out. Press. Pin and stitch the open edges together.

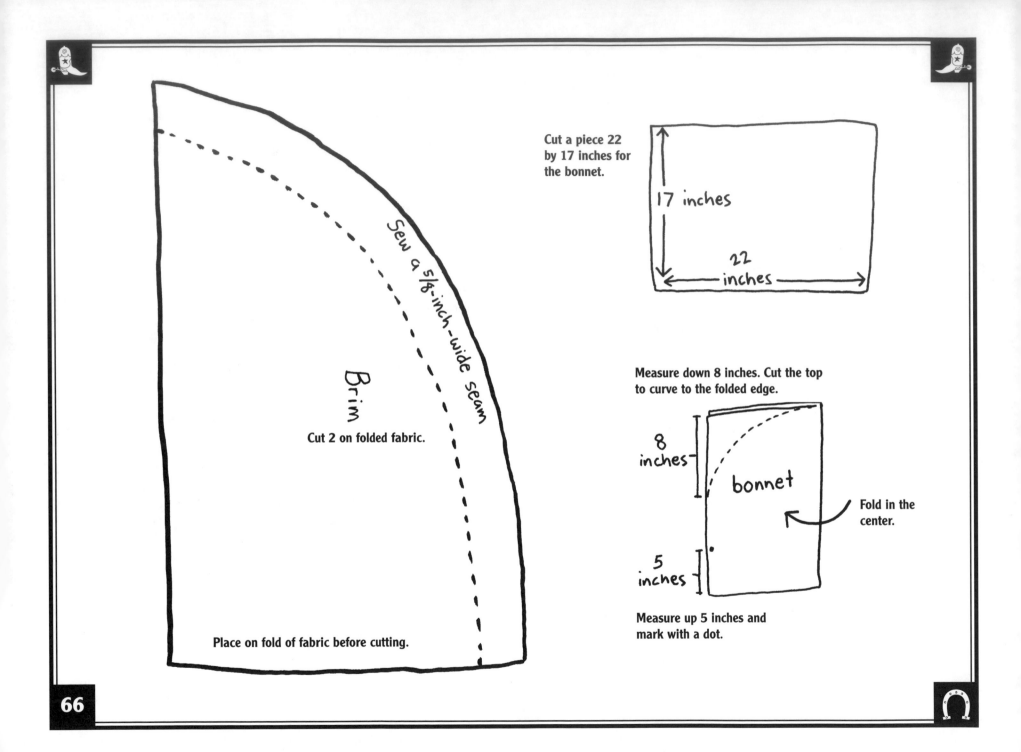

Sew a 5/8-inch-wide seam

Brim

Cut 2 on folded fabric.

Place on fold of fabric before cutting.

Cut a piece 22 by 17 inches for the bonnet.

17 inches

22 inches

Measure down 8 inches. Cut the top to curve to the folded edge.

8 inches

bonnet

Fold in the center.

5 inches

Measure up 5 inches and mark with a dot.

Turn the brim right side out. Press it flat with a steam iron. Pin the open edges together. Stitch the open ends together with long hand stitches along the edge to hold the pieces together.

Using a needle and thread, gather the bonnet piece along the curved edge between the dots. Adjust the bonnet gathers to fit the edge of the brim by pulling up on the ends of the thread. Pin the pieces together. Sew a ⅝-inch-wide seam.

Using a needle and thread, gather the back of the bonnet, between the dots, to make the bonnet fit the back of your head. Try it on to adjust the gathers for a good fit. Tie the threads in a knot and clip them.

Hem the back edge of the bonnet by turning under ¼-inch along the raw edge and stitching by hand or machine.

Cut 2 lengths of ribbon, each 18 inches long. Sew the ends of the ribbon to the sides of the bonnet below the brim. Trim the ends of the ribbons on a slant, to keep them from unraveling. Tie the ribbons under your neck.

Gather the bonnet along the curved edge.

Pull up the gathers to fit the brim. Stitch the seam. Make long gathering stitches between the dots you marked 5 inches from the edge.

hem

Pull up the threads so it fits the back of your neck. Knot the ends. Hem the edges by turning and stitching. Sew on ribbons for tying.

Men and boys wore hats to shade their faces, too. Sometimes hats and bonnets weren't enough. Sun glaring off the white desert or off a field of snow could cause blindness. Some people wore glasses with blue or green glass held together in a wire frame or held in leather goggles. Others who didn't have protective eyeglasses rubbed charcoal around their eyes and on their nose—the black cut down the glare of the sun.

Hurry up and Wait!

After a family had readied the wagon, the teams of animals to pull it, and their supplies, they gathered at the jumping-off towns to join into large groups called *trains*. These wagon trains were large because that would make the trip safer. No one wanted to straggle across the unknown prairies alone. There was safety in numbers, families could help one another in emergencies, and going as a group meant they could hire a scout who knew the way. Once a large train was organized, the people elected officers and a council of judges. Travelers had rules to follow. But once they left town, there would be no police or sheriff to enforce the law. The officers and judges of the train were responsible for maintaining order and punishing those who broke the rules.

Wagons were grouped into two divisions, each with a captain. The divisions were grouped into platoons, with four wagons in each platoon. This helped keep track of all family members and made it easier to organize the train in the morning and evening.

The council hired a guide, usually an old mountain man who could find the trail and who could select good spots to camp each evening. He would also give advice when problems arose.

Once they had decided to go and had everything ready, people were anxious to begin the long trip. But they couldn't leave whenever they wanted to. When travel depended on animals, as it did before trains and cars were common, trips had to be planned in advance. Animals needed to eat grass and drink water frequently along the way. Some grain was taken along for animal feed, but there was never enough for very long. That meant the wagon train's leaders had to schedule each day's travel, and scouts had to ride ahead looking for suitable places where the oxen and horses could graze and drink water. Trails were often longer because they went between watering and feeding spots, rather than straight across the land.

The animals' need for fresh grass meant that the early trains each spring had to wait at Independence or Westport until the grass had grown enough for grazing. They also had to wait until the snow had melted in the mountains, so there would be grass growing there when they passed through. That wait often meant they would be dangerously late getting over the mountains in Oregon and California if winter came early. Sometimes military units planted grass seed along trails and roads so their horses could find feed there later when they needed to travel that way again.

The huge number of wagons heading west made it difficult to find enough grass for all the animals. When more than five thousand wagons left each spring it became very important to be one of the early divisions to leave. Those who came later found all the pasture had been grazed down.

The buffalo grazed on the same grass, in huge herds that roamed the Plains. The travelers were glad to hunt them in order to get fresh meat, and they killed many. There seemed to be so many buffalo that people thought they could never be wiped out. Later, when hunters killed the herds for their hides, the animals nearly disappeared.

The Native North Americans watched the long trains of wagons rolling past, too. They had never seen so many strange people. They wondered where they had all come from, and told each other that there couldn't possibly be any people left in the East, so many had come into the West. They worried as they watched the newcomers graze their animals on the buffalo range and shoot wild animals they had depended on for food. Some Indians were eager to sell or trade with the travelers, but their coming made many other Indians angry, too.

When the wagons went down steep hills, the driver set the brake and locked the wheels so they wouldn't turn by putting a pole through the spokes of each set of wheels. Sometimes they tied a huge log to the back of the wagon to slow it even more. Without these precautions, because the hills were steep, the wagons could pick up speed, roll over the horses, and crash. Wagons usually had to be driven straight up and down hills, never sideways. The wheels weren't flexible on hillsides, and the wagon would tip over sideways too easily.

Day by Day

Once the train set out, everyday life was sort of dull. Each morning the boys helped hitch the teams to the wagons while girls helped cook breakfast over a campfire. By seven o'clock everyone was packed up and in line. When the bugle sounded they shouted, "Wagons, roll!" and everyone pulled out. The lead wagon from the day before went to the end of the line, so everyone had a chance to have a day in the front, without the choking dust.

At midday they stopped for a break they called *nooning*. The animals were able to rest, eat, and drink water. People ate a simple meal, then napped or did chores. Some mended clothing, others gathered firewood or buffalo chips for making the evening campfire. (On the plains there were no trees, so travelers gathered dried buffalo dung or grass and burned it for fuel.)

After about two hours, everyone got back in line and the caravan continued traveling until evening. Children took turns riding in the wagons or walking alongside. The wagons moved slowly, so people walked along looking for berries and firewood as they traveled.

About an hour before they were ready to camp for the night a few scouts were sent to ride ahead and look for a good camping spot. They needed a place that was big enough for all the wagons and animals, had wood for campfires, and water and grass for the animals. One of the scouts marked out a large circle, about one hundred yards across (that's as long as a football field). When the wagons got there they went around the circle until all were in place. Then they unyoked the oxen and let them graze inside the circle. Horses were tethered with ropes to stakes pounded into the ground. People hooked up chains between each wagon, to keep the animals from wandering out of the circle.

While the men and boys took care of the wagons and animals, the women and girls put up tents, built campfires, and cooked the evening meal. Some nights there wasn't much time to cook, and everyone was so tired that they might only have mush and milk. Milk came from the milk cow many families kept tied to the back of their wagon. At daybreak, about four A.M., the wagon leader sounded the trumpet and everyone woke for another day of travel.

Wagons traveled about fifteen to twenty miles per day. The trip was about two thousand miles to Oregon or California. Some days, when crossing rivers, canyons, or steep mountain passes, they traveled only one mile.

There were so many travelers that the wagon wheels wore deep ruts into the ground. After the first few years the Oregon Trail was so clearly worn that people no longer needed guides to show the way. They could simply follow the ruts and discarded trash that marked the way. People could even buy guide books for the trip before they left home.

Cross a River—With Triangles!

How did travelers know how long a rope was needed to stretch across a river in order to pull wagons across? Some just guessed, and often that meant sending a man across several times to try out different lengths of rope that might be lost in the crossing. Others used a traveler's guidebook that told how to do it mathematically, before even setting foot into the water. This method uses triangles.

Materials

Pencil

Paper

Ruler

Draw this on paper a few times, to see how it works. Then try it outdoors, using a long cord tied to wooden stakes so you can mark out straight lines. Pace with your feet to measure the distances. Count your steps as you go, measure 1 step with a ruler, then multiply the number of steps by the length of 1 step to find the distance.

1. You want to find out how far it is from point 1 to point 2, in order to cross the river. You are at point 1.

2. Draw a straight line from point 1 to point 2, then to point 3. The line from point 1 to point 2 would be imaginary across a real river.

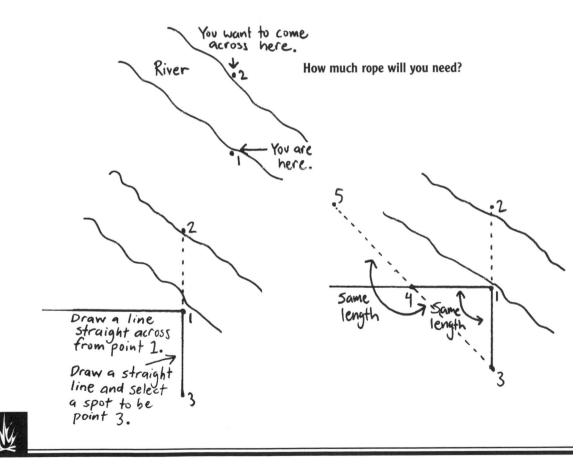

You want to come across here.

River

How much rope will you need?

You are here.

Draw a line straight across from point 1.

Draw a straight line and select a spot to be point 3.

Same length

Same length

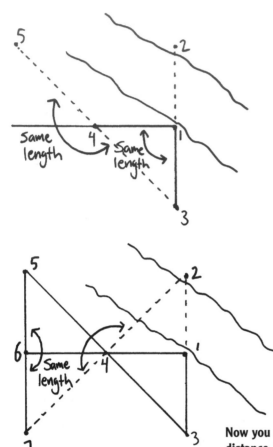

3. Extend a straight line out from point 1 to the side, at a right angle. Mark point 4 the same distance from point 1 as point 3 is.

4. Make a line from point 3 to meet the line at point 4.

5. Measure the length of that line, and go out from point 4 the same distance to create point 5.

6. Measure the distance from point 1 to point 4 and draw a line out the same length to create point 6.

7. Draw a straight line from point 5 to point 6 and extend it.

8. Measure the distance from point 5 to point 6. Measure the same distance from point 6 to point 7.

9. Now you can measure the distance between point 6 and point 7. It will be the same length as from point 1 to point 2. That's how far it will be to cross the river.

This seems like a lot of work, but after a few times, the wagon master and his assistants could quickly pace off the distances and set stakes in the ground, then measure and be ready to *ford* the river. Fording is crossing a river in a shallow part by wading.

Now you can see that triangles have measured the distance. This is called *triangulation* and is a way to measure land.

The distance from point 1 to point 2 will be the same as from point 6 to point 7. Measure between point 6 and point 7—that's how long the rope must be (at least!).

Ropes were used many times a day, and quickly wore out or were lost. Sometimes travelers traded Native North Americans for their hide ropes, but discovered that wolves ate through hide ropes and set animals loose at night. Hemp or cotton ropes were best.

Eating and Drinking

Travelers drank muddy water from ponds and rivers. They would sometimes stretch a handkerchief over a cup and drink the water, letting the handkerchief strain out the dirt and animal matter. People then didn't know that germs caused sickness. They didn't know that the dirty water made them sick—they usually thought it was stagnant air that caused fevers.

Alkaline water (water containing salt) was dangerous to horses and oxen that drank it. It poisoned and killed them. Even grass growing near alkali water caused sickness. Travelers sometimes treated their animals who had become sick from alkali poisoning by pouring a bucket of grease down their throat, or by mixing a bucket of flour and water and letting the animal drink it. Alkali water was found in Wyoming, Nevada, and California.

The people who brought a milk cow along could milk the cow, skim off the cream, and fill a butter churn with the cream. The cream would shake into butter as the wagon bounced along over the trail.

As they traveled, people fished and hunted for other food. They fished in streams for trout and bluegill. They hunted quail and doves. They made meals of beaver tail, roast dog, panther, prairie dogs, mountain sheep, and even horse meat.

Pioneers brought honeybees west with them. They kept the hives wrapped up, sometimes under a bed in the wagon. Honeybees didn't live in the West until settlers brought them.

Johnnycakes

Johnnycakes, sometimes called journey cakes, were very popular across the West. Travelers as well as settlers could make them from corn, which was easy to grow or purchase from Native North American farmers.

Ingredients

2 eggs

1 cup water

3/4 cup milk

2 tablespoons oil

1 teaspoon salt

2 cups yellow cornmeal

Butter

Maple syrup

Utensils

Bowl

Spoon

Griddle or frying pan

Pancake turner

(Adult help suggested.)
Mix the eggs, water, milk, oil, and salt together in a bowl. Stir in the cornmeal. Stir it until all the lumps are smooth. Heat the griddle. Put a bit of oil on the griddle to keep the cakes from sticking. Pour 1/4 cup (about two tablespoons) of batter onto the hot griddle. Fry the cake until it's done on 1 side, then turn it over and cook the other. Eat johnnycakes warm with butter and syrup. This recipe makes about 12 cakes.

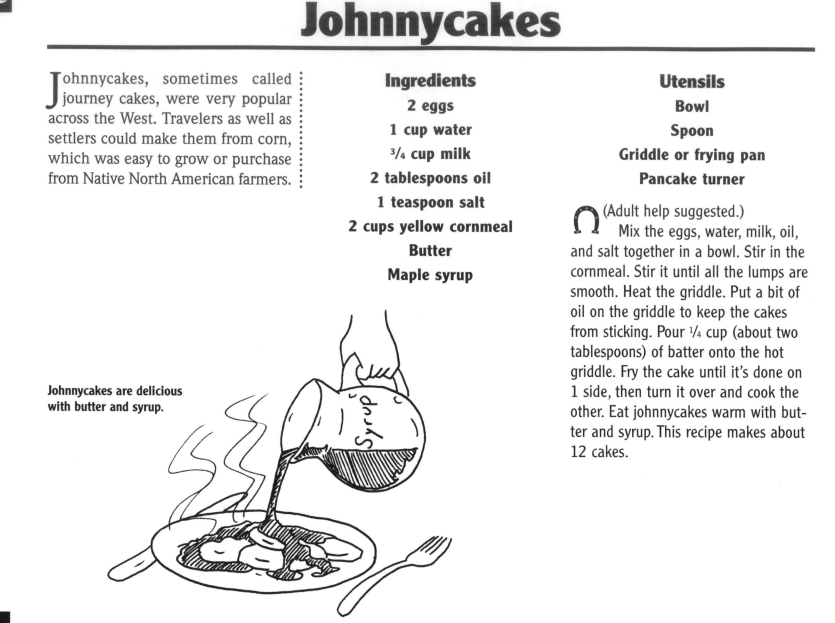

Johnnycakes are delicious with butter and syrup.

Bullwhacker

Because oxen were driven along without reins or ropes (their necks were held in a wooden yoke), people would walk along beside them, pulling on the yoke to guide the oxen. In a wagon train, oxen followed along after the wagon in front and needed to be prodded to keep moving. For that, a whip was used. When snapped it made a cracking sound. The loud crack of the whip in the air over their heads reminded the animals to keep moving. Yelling helped, too. Practice your skill with a whip playing this game.

Materials

Rope (cotton or nylon), 10 feet long and ½-inch thick

Stick, about 6 inches long

Coin

Poke the stick into the ground and place the coin on top of the stick. Now, stand back and, using the rope like a whip, try to knock the coin off without knocking the stick over.

Try to knock the coin off the stick without knocking the stick over.

Not every day went smoothly. Sometimes wagons broke down and everyone waited while they were repaired. A horse or child might be missing, and everyone stopped to look. No one was left behind. People quarreled, families fought with each other—just as people always do. Others became good friends, and many families who met on the wagon trains later settled near one another. Many children who met during the trip later married each other.

Stealing Sticks Game

Traveling for months got pretty boring for everyone, but there were ways to have fun, too. This game was played by children when the wagons were stopped for nooning, while waiting to cross a flooded river, or while waiting for hunters to bring back meat or lost mules and oxen. A Mormon girl traveling to Utah wrote about playing this game in her travel diary.

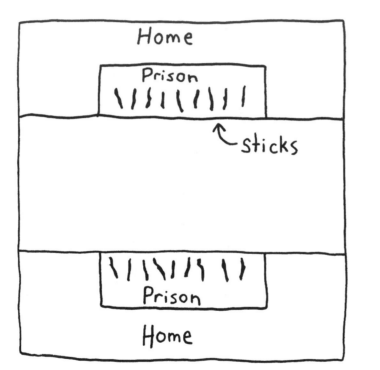

Lay out the playing field like this. Spread the sticks out in the prisons.

Materials

Playing field

4–6 sticks for each side

Players for 2 teams, at least 6 on each side

Divide the players into two equal teams. Line out the playing field so it has two lines about 30- to 60-feet apart. Mark an area at each end, about 6 by 10 feet, to be each team's prison.

Place an equal number of sticks on the ground in each prison. Space them out across the length of the prison.

Begin the game by one side sending out a player to dare the opponents to tag her. One of the enemy starts to chase her and she runs for home. Home is the safe area behind the line. If she is tagged before she can make it to home, she is a prisoner and must immediately go over and stand in the enemy's prison. She goes there alone, because the one who tagged her gets chased by another player from her team, who goes into the playing field. Players try to run across the field and free prisoners held by the other side. If the player who runs across tags a prisoner, she is free. Prisoners need keep only 1 foot inside the prison, so it is easier to tag their hands. A team must rescue all its players who are being held in prison before they can steal any of the sticks held there. If there are no players in prison, the players try to take 1 stick at a time back to their home. Players can't be tagged on the way back home with a stick.

The first team to take all of the sticks from the other team wins.

People faced not only hardships on the trail, but sometimes tragic conditions. Here's what one girl wrote in the spring of 1847:

The past winter has seen a strange fever raging here. It seems to be contagious and it is raging terribly. Nothing seems to stop it but to tear up and take a six-month trip across the Plains with ox teams to the Pacific Ocean.

Trail Hardships

The overland trip was not easy. No matter how careful people were, they had accidents and became sick during the trip. Children and adults fell from the slow moving wagons and were crushed beneath the heavy wheels. Some drowned trying to swim across rivers. People got sick from drinking bad water or milk from cows that ate poison weeds. Most of the people who died during the trip west became ill from diseases for which there was no cure at that time such as typhoid, mountain fever, dysentery, cholera, flu, measles, and smallpox.

Many people were afraid of attacks by angry North American Indians and feared death in this way, but most people who died during the trip died from accident or disease. The Indians caught the diseases, too. The germs were on clothing, blankets, trade goods, and food. Thousands of Indians died from disease, sometimes whole villages at once.

There were attacks by bandits, too. Sometimes they were North American Indians, sometimes whites dressed up as Indians. Helpless travelers had their horses, food, and equipment stolen by thieves who sold the items to the next train passing through.

It wasn't easy. Disease, attacks, little grass or water, and harsh weather made it difficult. As the trip wore on, the oxen and horses grew tired and weaker. The supplies gave out. Then people became desperate for food. They began to toss out heavy items—furniture, clothing, tools—to lighten the load for the weak animals. By the middle of the trip the trail was scattered with people's discards. Piles of clothing and blankets, wooden barrels, chests, stoves, tools, and mirrors marked the path of litter across the plains. Those who took too many things or useless luxuries were the first to begin lightening their load. Sometimes people who lived at a nearby fort followed along behind the trains at a distance, waiting for travelers to begin throwing away their possessions.

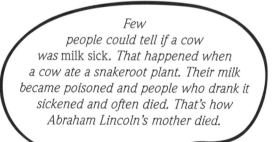

Few people could tell if a cow was milk sick. That happened when a cow ate a snakeroot plant. Their milk became poisoned and people who drank it sickened and often died. That's how Abraham Lincoln's mother died.

As people in the train ran out of food supplies they began to barter with each other. Precious dishes and fancy items were of no value—everyone wanted a sack full of beans instead!

Not everyone traveled in a covered wagon. Many people built wooden handcarts (like large wheelbarrows) and pulled or pushed them along the way. Some walked and led a pack mule. Others just walked with a pack on their back—even children. During the later years of the Oregon Trail, wealthy families went west in fancy carriages with a full-time cook, a real stove, and several wagons full of supplies. Some even had huge two-story wagons built!

No matter the hardship, people still had fun on the way. They marveled at the towering Rocky Mountains and the herds of buffalo that carpeted the plains. They saw bubbling springs of soda water, hot springs, and ice caves. They saw more country than they had ever seen in their lives. It was a time of excitement and wonder. The first wagon train of nine hundred people in 1843 started an era. By 1869, when railroads made the trip faster and easier, about three hundred thousand people had left Missouri for the West.

You can still find the Oregon Trail in parts of western states. In Kansas and Nebraska it has been plowed into farm fields, but in Wyoming the wheel ruts are still there—more than three hundred miles of them! There's also a special museum in Baker, Oregon—the National Historic Oregon Trail Interpretive Center.

About twenty thousand people died on the Oregon Trail, about ten deaths for each mile of the route. So many animals perished from exhaustion, lack of food and water, or alkali poisoning from bad water, that the trail was lined with bones in some areas. One man wrote that he held his nose to count 150 dead oxen in one spot.

It wasn't cowboys or gunfighters that opened the West, but farmers and their families. If they hadn't gone West, the United States might never have expanded to the Pacific. Most of those who went West were well-to-do landowners and business owners who sold their property to go to a better climate with no malaria, no slavery, and more opportunities. They were willing to risk everything for a better life. If Lewis and Clark, fur traders, and wagon trains hadn't settled the West, Britain and Mexico might have kept it, and perhaps only Native North Americans would have lived there.

People who traveled the trails had a saying about "seeing the elephant." Seeing the elephant *meant any great experience. They meant they were going to see what was there at the end of the journey. If someone asked why you were traveling, you might tell them "to see the elephant." People who got disgusted and turned back told others on the way back that they had seen the elephant.*

SETTLING DOWN

Travelers who went West by wagon usually settled in California or Oregon, but many went to other places, too. Some liked the looks of land along the way, and settled along the Oregon Trail. Some settled down to build a home before getting to where they wanted to go—they were out of money, or their supplies and animals were gone, and they could go no further. When the best land had been taken up in California and Oregon, settlers looked other places. They spread out across the mountains and prairies, settling near rivers or forests first so they would have drinking water and logs for a house. Others headed to the grassy prairies, where they had to find their own water and build houses without logs because there were no trees.

In 1862, Congress passed the Homestead Act, which gave 160 acres of land to unmarried adults or heads of households. That meant men or women could be homesteaders. One-hundred and sixty acres seemed like a lot of land to people in the East, where farms of that size could be successful. But once they got to the West, settlers discovered that the land was rocky, dry, had poor soil, or was subject to harsh weather. The cows and horses needed many more acres to graze on the thin grass. People homesteaded 160 acres, then usually bought more from neighbors or the railroad and canal companies, who were given large pieces of western land by the government in exchange for building railroads and canals. Land cost about four dollars an acre at that time. Railroads were eager to sell their land, and advertised the land in the East and Europe. They hired recruiters and guides who brought groups of Europeans out to the West to buy land and build homes.

Measuring and Marking Land

Homesteaders needed to measure out and mark the land they were claiming or buying. In order to do that, a method was created to measure land. Land in the United States is measured in this way today, too.

All measurements were taken from *latitude* and *longitude* markings. These are invisible lines on the earth, invented by people to help them measure distance. You can find them drawn on a globe of the world. Can you find the nearest line to where you live? Land between these lines is divided into imaginary *townships*. Each township is a square six miles in each direction. A township is divided into thirty-six sections. Each section was one mile each direction—that's 640 acres. Each section was numbered (see the

36	30	24	18	12	6
35	29	23	17	11	5
34	28	22	16	10	4
33	27	21	15	9	3
32	26	20	14	8	2
31	25	19	13	7	1

6 miles

6 miles

This is how a township is divided. Each square is 1 mile across and is called a Section.

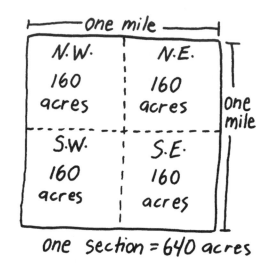

one mile

one mile

one section = 640 acres

Each section is divided into quarter sections of 160 acres each. Quarter sections are located by their position in a section: northwest quarter, northeast quarter, southwest quarter, or southeast quarter. Can you locate 160 acres in the southwest quarter of Section 16? That's how homesteaders described their land claim.

drawing). Sections were divided into four units of 160 acres each. These were called *quarter sections*. A homesteader would check with the Land Office in the nearest town and locate a quarter section he or she wanted to file a claim on. Then the homesteaders had to go out and locate the claimed land, mark the corners, and file papers so no one else would claim it.

People could mark the corners of sections and quarter sections by driving posts into the ground. People also marked section corners by marking a *witness tree*. A witness tree is the nearest tree to a corner which has been *blazed* (a patch of bark sliced away with an ax). The number of the range, township and section number were then carved into the blaze with a knife.

Once homesteaders had located their land and marked the corners of the 160-acre claim, they needed to get busy and build a house. Part of the homestead rule was that the homesteader had to build a house and live in it for five years to gain title to the land.

People built their first house very simple and rough—planning to build a grander home after they cleared and plowed the rest of their homestead into farmland. They took the wheels off of the wagon and

lived in it or in tents while they worked on a quick and simple house. After the house was built, the wagon bed could be used as a storage shed or extra bedroom.

Settlers built simple cabins which were all one room. There wasn't a kitchen; all cooking was done at the fireplace or outside. Later a *lean-to* (an extension or shed) was built on the outside of the cabin for a cook-stove and kitchen. There were no separate bedrooms; everyone slept in the one room. There wasn't a bathroom either. People took a bath once in a while in a large metal tub set up in front of the fireplace. *Outhouses*, little houses set over holes dug in the ground, were used for bathrooms before flushable toilets were invented.

It was pretty easy to build a cabin from logs. The logs were stacked on top of each other and notches were cut into the ends so the logs would fit together. The cracks between the logs were filled with wet clay or moss—a job for the children, usually. Rocks were gathered and stacked to make a fireplace against the wall of the cabin. Wet clay or a mixture called *cat and clay* was used to hold the rocks in place. Cat and clay was a mixture of cattail fluff and soft clay soil. When it dried, the fireplace was solid. People sometimes made wallpaper by gluing newspapers to the inside walls. The newspapers could be painted white with whitewash made from *lime*. Lime was made by burning limestone or clam shells, then mixing it with water.

Pretty wallpaper could be made by painting designs on the newspaper, making it look like fancy paper or marble.

Pillows were made from sacks full of pine needles or grass. Newspaper made a tablecloth. Dishes were usually of tin—it was cheap and didn't break.

Many people built houses and even forts from *adobe* (say it: uh-doe-bee) blocks. Adobe was made from a mixture of clay and straw. Blocks were made by filling wooden forms with wet adobe. The forms were removed and the bricks of adobe dried in the sun. When dry, they could be stacked up like bricks. If you travel in the Southwest today, you can still see a few old adobe buildings. Early settlers in wet climates tried building with what they called *'dobe* (say it: dough-bee), but the wet winter weather soon ruined the clay blocks.

Limestone is a rock made of ancient sea animals. If you find some on the ground, it means you have located an area that was once under water. Test a rock to see if it is limestone. Sprinkle it with lemon juice or vinegar. If the juice fizzes and bubbles, it's limestone. The bubbling happens because acid in the juice makes the limestone give off carbon dioxide gas.

Home on the Plains

People who settled on the grassy plains had a problem, though. There were no trees to cut down for cabins, and no riverbanks where they could gather clay for adobe blocks. What could they use to build a house? They looked at the North American Indian houses that the Pawnee and Mandans made and saw they were built from dirt pressed over sticks. So they reached for their spades and began slicing into the thick grass growing all around them. The grass had thickly matted roots that went almost fifteen feet deep. The sod could be sliced into chunks that could be stacked up like bricks. People jokingly called these sod blocks "Nebraska marble," but they found that the houses made from them were not too bad. Some sod blocks were built even more quickly by digging into the side of a grassy hillside. It was sort of a cave with a roof built on. These were called *dugouts*. Some people hated living in dugouts, saying they were living underground like animals. Others liked their cozy little homes, especially when the roof was in bloom with spring wild-flowers.

A sod house (or *soddy*) was easy to build and cheap—it only cost about thirteen dollars and seventy-five cents to build one in Nebraska. That bought a bit of lumber to frame a roof, a roll of tar paper for the ceiling, and a keg of nails.

Soddies were surprisingly snug and comfortable. The thick walls kept the inside warm in winter and cool in summer. People liked having a roof in bloom with sunflowers in spring. There was no danger the house would burn—even the fireplace could be built from blocks of sod.

But there were problems with living in a house made of dirt and grass. When it rained, it leaked badly. One woman told how she had cooked hotcakes during a rainstorm while her daughter held an umbrella over her—indoors! Dirt was always falling off the ceiling. Bugs, mice, and snakes would live in it, too. Sometimes a cow even fell through the roof of a dugout! Even with all the problems, most people lived in their soddy for about six or seven years.

There were other problems with living on the plains, too. There was no wood to burn for heating or cooking. People gathered buffalo chips to burn at first, but soon the buffalo had been killed and there weren't enough buffalo chips. They gathered chips from their own cattle and burned cornstalks and corn cobs from their fields. They even burned grass.

Children spent a great deal of time gathering grass to burn in winter. Because dry grass burns quickly they had to gather immense amounts of it. The dry grass was twisted and tied in a tight loop so it would burn more slowly. Some people even bought special grass-burning stoves, but not everyone could afford them.

Some people rode horseback miles away to find cottonwood trees they could use for a roof frame which they covered with brush, grass, and more sod. Eventually sunflowers and grass grew on the roof. How pretty a house would be with the roof in full bloom!

The floor of a soddy was dirt, packed and polished with soapy water. (Imagine throwing the bathwater on the living room floor!) The door was made from a piece of canvas or leather. If a family did have a wooden door, they could use a leather shoe sole nailed on for a hinge.

Here's an old song from the time called "The Little Old Sod Shanty."

I am looking rather seedy now while holding down my claim

And my victuals are not always served the best,

And the mice play shyly round me as I nestle down to rest,

In my little old sod shanty in the West.

The hinges are of leather and the windows have no glass

While the board roof lets the howling blizzards in,

And I hear the hungry coyote as he slinks up through the grass

Round my little old sod shanty on my claim.

Oiled Paper Windows

Some settlers had enough money to buy glass windows for their soddy, but many used pieces of hide or oiled paper for windows. Try this project to see how oiled paper becomes *translucent*—that means see-through.

Materials

Brown paper grocery bag

Scissors

Salad oil

Paper towel

Newspapers

Cut open a brown grocery sack, then cut a section small enough to work with, about 12 by 12 inches. Use a paper towel to spread salad oil on the newspaper. Cover both sides. Wipe it with a dry paper towel. Hold it up to a window, and you'll see that it lets light through. Compare it to a piece of paper that hasn't been oiled. See the difference? People in soddies didn't have salad oil; they would have used lard, made from cooked animal fat.

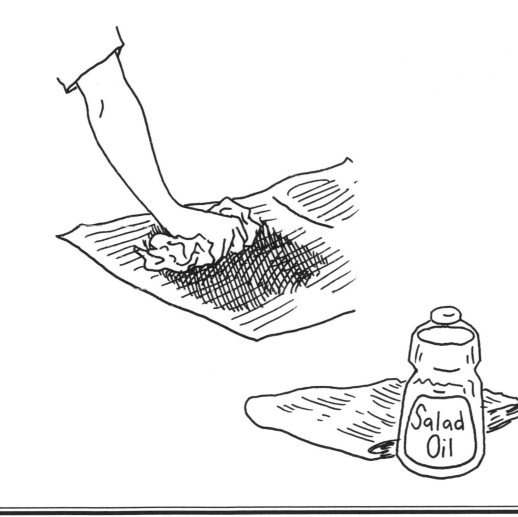

Dowse for Water

Water for people and animals was another problem for settlers all over the West. The first homesteaders took up the land along the streams and rivers, so those who came later had to settle away from these water sources. Those who didn't live too far from the stream hauled water in barrels in a wagon. But most settlers were too far from water for that. They had to dig wells. That had been easy enough to do in the East where a shovel and bucket could be used to dig a deep hole. But in many places in the West the water was more than one hundred feet below the surface. That meant hiring a well driller with a steam powered drill. This was very costly, so people wanted to be sure they were drilling in a spot where water was likely to be underground.

People known as *switchers* traveled around the country locating underground water for people. They were also called *dowsers* and would dowse for water. They would search for underground water by walking around holding a forked stick or wire out in front of them. If water was beneath the ground, they claimed the stick (called a *water witch*) would mysteriously pull toward the ground. Water switchers claimed a high skill and were paid well. They didn't always locate water, but when they did people were grateful.

Materials
Forked stick, about 2 feet long (dowsers claim hazel or willow wood are best)

or

Wire coat hanger

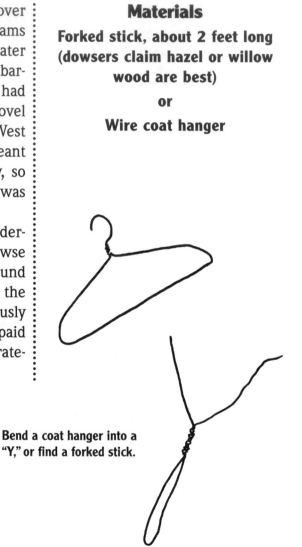

Bend a coat hanger into a "Y," or find a forked stick.

Unwrap the twisted ends of the coat hanger and bend it into a "Y" shape. Hold the 2 ends of the forked stick or the wire, and hold the other end out in front of you. Walk slowly, holding the wire steady. Watch the end and you should see it begin to bend or quiver if you are standing over underground water. Try it, and see if you think it works. Some dowsers even claimed to be able to locate buried treasure!

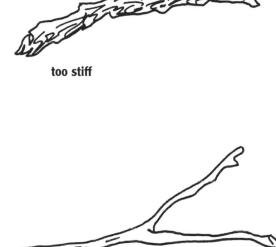

too stiff

more flexible is better

Hold the stick steady and watch it. Dowsers say it will dip down toward underground water.

Windlass

Once the water well was dug or drilled, settlers needed to get the water up out of the ground. If the well wasn't too deep they could lower a bucket on a rope, then pull it back up. For deeper wells, a windlass was used to wind the rope up and down.

Materials

1-quart milk carton

Plastic drinking straw

Small paper ketchup cup (save from a fast-food restaurant)

String

Scissors

Large nail

Small rock to weight the bucket

Cut off the top of the carton and cut a window in every side so you can watch the windlass work. Use a large nail to work 2 holes in the sides, about 1 inch from the top. Make them directly across from each other and large enough to fit the straw through and allow it to turn freely. Slide the straw in place through the holes.

Work 2 holes across from each other in the sides of the ketchup container and tie a piece of string through them to make a handle. It will be the bucket.

Cut a piece of string about 18 inches long and tie it around the center of the straw. Tie the other end to the bucket handle. Roll the straw to wind the string around the straw. Place a small rock inside the bucket to keep it from tipping over. Fill the bottom of the milk carton with about 3 inches of water. Now you can lower the bucket by turning the straw, letting it drop to the bottom and fill with water. Bring it back up by turning the straw to wind the string up.

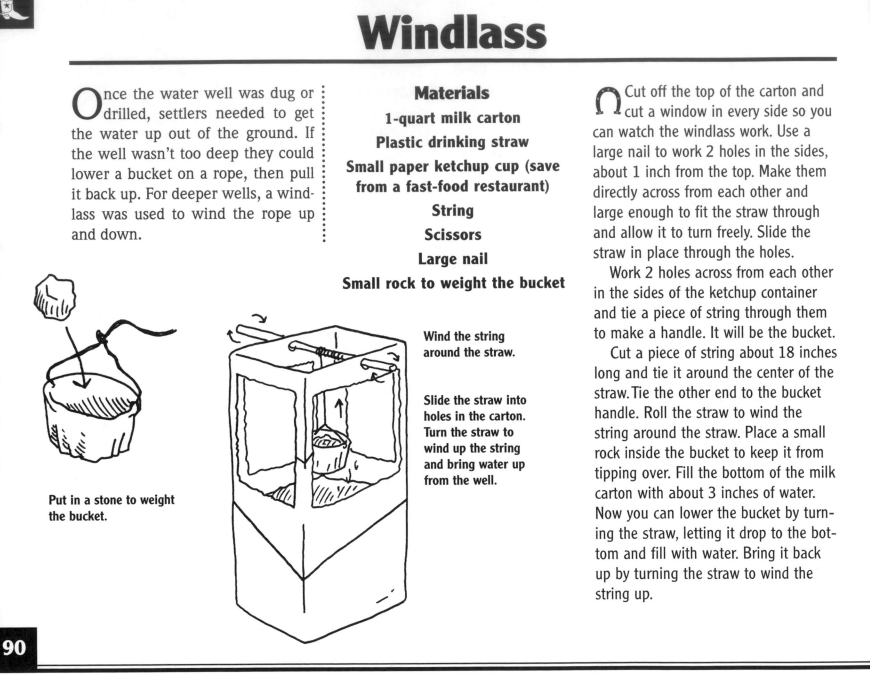

Put in a stone to weight the bucket.

Wind the string around the straw.

Slide the straw into holes in the carton. Turn the straw to wind up the string and bring water up from the well.

Windmill

Pulling buckets of water up the well was easy enough, unless the well was over one hundred feet deep or there were other chores to do. It could take all day to bring up enough water—and there was plenty of other work to be done. Windmills had been used in Europe for centuries since the Arabs invented them in A.D. 644. When settlers from Europe reached the West they looked around and noticed there seemed to be plenty of wind, so they set to work building windmills to pump water. The sails of the windmills in Europe were built of cloth, but Americans built them from steel, which was cheaper and more durable.

Because the prairie wind doesn't blow all the time (only about eight hours out of every twenty-four), a storage tank held water so there would always be a supply. Windmills were used to grind corn and power sawmills, too. There's still plenty of wind today, and windmills are being used to create electricity in many places in the West.

Settlers could make working windmills from old wagon axles, wooden coffee boxes, and scrap iron for about one dollar and fifty cents. Here's a simple project you can make that lets you see how wind can turn a windmill.

Materials

Typing paper

Construction paper

Ruler

Pencil

Scissors

Drinking straw

Straight pin

Trace the square on the following page onto a piece of typing paper. Cut out the square, place it on top of a piece of construction paper, and trace. Cut this square out. Cut from each corner into the middle of the square, being careful not to cut through the center. Fold the paper to the right

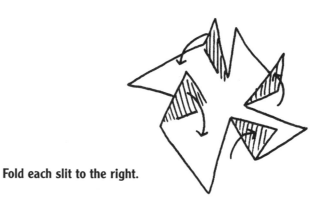

Fold each slit to the right.

along each slit. Push the straight pin through the center of the paper and into the end of a drinking straw. Bend the sharp end of the pin down to secure it. Now blow on the windmill and watch it spin!

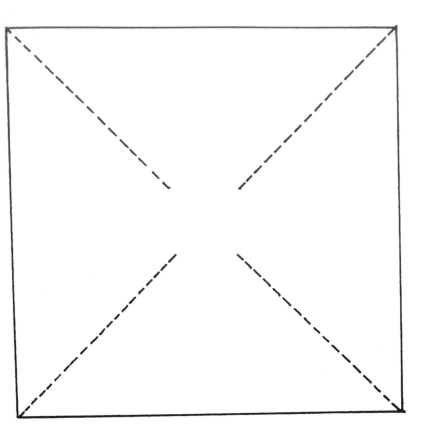

Cut a square. Make slits from the corners into the middle.

Pin to a straw or pencil eraser.
Blow and the wind will spin the wheel.

Set Some Type

Building a house was one of the requirements for getting homestead land. *Proving-up notices* was something else that had to be done. Homesteaders had to pay the nearest newspaper to print notices that they had claimed their land. The notices told where the land was using the township and section numbers. This was so everyone knew what land was being claimed. Since everyone who homesteaded had to pay to get these notices printed, people started printing a lot of newspapers. One newspaper didn't carry much news, but it listed two hundred proving-up notices. People had to pay five or six dollars for a notice to be printed. Newspapers made a good profit. Some newspaper editors carried a printing press from town to town in a wagon, moving to newly homesteaded areas just to print the notices.

Printing newspapers was a lot of work. Tiny letters were made of metal, and each one had to be set in place in a row. Once all the letters were set for a page, the page was printed. Afterward, the letters were all taken out and reset for the next page.

Do what a pioneer newspaper editor did; set a page of type and print it!

Materials
Alphabet pasta, uncooked

4-by-8-inch piece of heavy cardboard

Glue

Toothpick

Ink, tempera paint, or watercolor marking pens

Paper to print on

Decide what you want to print first. Start with your name, then add more as you get better at it. Here's

Position the pasta letters on the glue. Remember, everything must be backward! When the glue is dry, color the letters with markers or paint.

the difficult part—each line must be printed backward, and each letter must be placed backward! Put the letters down 1 at a time on the cardboard and glue them in place. Use a toothpick to straighten them. When the glue is dry, ink or paint the letters and press them against the paper. Press the paper firmly with your fingers to be sure to get a good impression. Print as many copies as you want.

Newspapers back then didn't look exactly like newspapers today. There were no photographs; instead, drawings were printed from woodblocks or etchings. Artists drew on plates of metal, cutting lines into the surface to create the illustration.

One problem for frontier newspapers was getting enough paper. When shipments from the East were delayed, they printed newspapers on whatever was handy—wrapping paper, wallpaper, and even cloth.

Press the letters onto paper to print.

Women typesetters, editors, and even publishers were common in the West—unthinkable jobs for women in the East at the time.

MANDY

Print an Engraving

Here's a project you can try that involves printing an etched plate, the same way early newspaper illustrations were printed. Print on copy paper or try wallpaper, shopping bags, or cloth—just like they sometimes had to do on the frontier!

Materials

Styrofoam tray (save from bakery goods, or use Styrofoam plate or top lid of Styrofoam egg carton)

Ball-point pen

Tempera paint

Pan and brush for paint

Paper

Newspapers

Cover the work area with newspapers. Use the pen to draw designs or images on the Styrofoam tray. Press firmly so it cuts a line into the surface. When you are finished drawing, cover the whole surface of the tray with paint. Brush the paint on with a brush until the tray is coated with a light coat of paint.

Place the paper you want to print with on top of the painted tray and press it firmly against the Styrofoam design. Rub the paper gently with your fingers to be sure the design gets printed. Pull the paper gently away from the printing surface and let it dry. Make as many prints as you want, repainting the surface of the engraving between prints.

Press the design lines into the Styrofoam.

Spread the paint. Press the paper onto the design to make a print.

Save a Seed

Homesteaders had to work quickly getting everything done. They built the house, a barn, and corrals for the animals. They plowed the land with a hand plow pulled by a horse or an ox. Most of them planted crops they had experience with such as rye, barley, wheat, and corn. They had brought the seed with them in large sacks. They planted potatoes, using cut up potatoes they had brought along in the wagon, too. People saved the seeds from foods they ate, then planted them when they reached the West.

Materials

Seeds saved from a snack: apple, pear, orange, grape, pumpkin, squash, or watermelon seeds

Small pot

Soil

This project will take time, perhaps months in the case of the apple and pear seeds. Save a few seeds and let them dry for a few days. Plant them about 1 inch deep in a small pot of soil. Put the pot in a sunny windowsill. Keep the soil moist but not too wet. Eventually you'll see a tiny plant emerge. When it gets 2 sets of leaves it's ready to transplant into the garden.

Keep the plant in a sunny window.

Mock Oysters

Settlers were so far from stores and they had so little money that they had to make nearly everything they needed. They sometimes missed foods they had enjoyed back East and tried to make *mock foods* (foods that looked and tasted like the real thing) to take their place. Clever cooks tried to make treats such as apple pie made from crushed crackers, mock mincemeat made from pumpkin and grapes chopped and soaked in vinegar, or mock oysters made from corn, eggs, and butter. Even coffee was sometimes hard to come by, so people settled for brews made from other things they had. They made a coffee-type drink from burnt barley, okra seeds, carrots or cornmeal, and molasses. Very few coffee drinkers in the West ever tasted a real coffee bean! Most families had a coffee grinder, but used it to grind corn or wheat. Hot water and ground-up roasted dried corn was a very popular drink which was very similar to today's Postum drink.

Oysters were one of the most popular foods in the old West, if you could get them. Since most people couldn't buy or trade for them, or raise them on the farm, they tried to make a substitute.

Ingredients

1 can (15-ounce) whole kernel corn

$1/4$ cup milk

$1/3$ cup flour

1 egg

2 pinches salt

Pinch of pepper

2 tablespoons cooking oil

Utensils

Mixing bowl

Large spoon

Frying pan

Pancake turner

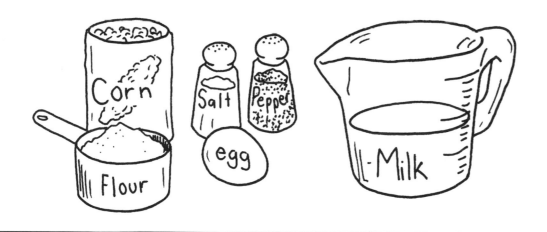

(Adult help suggested.)

Open the can of corn and drain the liquid away. Put the corn, milk, flour, egg, salt, and pepper in a mixing bowl. Mix together with a large spoon.

Heat the oil in a frying pan. Spoon small amounts of the corn mixture into the frying pan, making small cakes or mounds with the mixture. Fry the "oysters" on 1 side, then turn them over and fry the other side. When they are golden brown, remove them from the frying pan. Eat them while they are warm.

Cheap Ice Cream

Here's an old recipe for you to think about. Just imagine!

1 1/2 ounces Irish moss
1 gallon of milk

First soak the moss in a little cold water for an hour, and rinse well to clear it of sand and a certain peculiar taste; then steep it for an hour in the milk just to the boiling point, but not to boil; it imparts a rich color and flavor without eggs or cream. The moss may be steeped twice.

What Settlers Wore

People had to make their own clothing, too. There weren't any paper patterns for clothing until after the Civil War, so before that time women made patterns from lightweight cloth. They would also take apart old clothing and trace around the pieces to make new garments. Many people *turned* their clothing. That meant that the seams of the garments were carefully pulled apart and then the clothing was sewn back together, with the inside on the outside, so it could be worn longer.

People did want to be stylish, though, and they treasured fashion magazines from the cities. Women looked at the drawings and tried to copy the fashions for themselves and their family. They made fancy hats by weaving wheat straw and topping it with dried flowers. They made bustles—all the rage in the cities—by punching a hole in a tomato can and running a string through it. Tied on behind a woman's waist, it made her skirt puff out just right. People in even the smallest farm town or gold camp tried to dress fashionably. They thought fancy clothing showed that someone was successful and civilized. Laundry women often wore tight-fitting dressy shoes even if their feet hurt, and men wore white shirts, vests, and pocket watches (if they had them) even when doing hard work.

Men wore cuffs and collars made from stiff white paper. They buttoned them to their wrists, under the sleeves of their jackets and around their necks. That way a man looked like he was wearing a fresh white shirt, but he didn't have to launder one. The collars and cuffs were disposable, and were thrown away when they got too dirty. Men bought them in boxes of a dozen.

Shopping

With most people living too far from stores, peddlers and traders saw the opportunity to take the stores to the people. The first traders the settlers bargained with were North American Indians, who came to the settlers with food, moccasins, hides and fur robes, skin clothing, baskets, and beadwork for barter or sale. In the early days of western settlement the Indians wouldn't take money for these goods—they had nowhere to spend it so it was useless to them. They wanted iron cooking pots, well-made knives and fishhooks, needles, and sewing thread instead. Indians would also trade for beads, which they could use to decorate their clothing or for trade with other tribes. White settlers brought beads from the East to trade with Indians, or made beads themselves to trade.

Peddlers traveled across the plains and prairies, too. A peddler usually started with a few items in a pack on his back. Once he made some money and was able to afford it, peddlers bought a horse and wagon to ease their travels. Peddlers sold tree seedlings, early washing machines, clothing, pins, needles, buttons, thread, fabrics, ribbons and laces, and anything else that might catch the eye of a lonely family far from a store.

Shoppers had to be careful in those days. Many of the things sold in stores were fake or filled with things that cheated them and made more profit for the storekeeper. Whether they shopped in a city, town, or from a peddler, people found that sacks of coffee or tea were often filled with dark sand to make it heavy. White sugar often had cheap flour mixed into it. Even milk was mixed with chalk and water to cheat the customer.

Two Bits, Four Bits, Six Bits, a Dollar

What type of money was used in the West? Mostly Mexican coins at first. Because of that, people called coins *bits*. That's because in Mexico the old Spanish coins were called *pieces of eight*. They were broken down into eight *reales* or bits, as the Americans called them. Stores and peddlers didn't keep many coins on hand to make change. People were expected to spend even money: two bits (twenty-five cents), four bits (fifty cents), and six bits (seventy-five cents) were the amounts used. A bit was about twelve and one-half cents in Mexican money—so a dime was too little, and was called a *short bit*. The nickel wasn't minted until the 1890s.

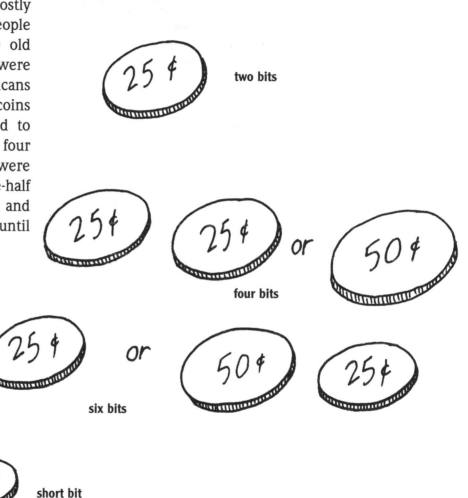

25 ¢   **two bits**

25¢   25¢   or   50¢   **four bits**

25¢   25¢   25¢   or   50¢   25¢   **six bits**

10¢   **short bit**

Impact on Animals

As more and more settlers made homes and farms in the wilderness, things began to change. The first animal to feel the effects of so many people moving into its territory was the passenger pigeon. There were once billions of passenger pigeons in North America. They migrated with the seasons, and when flocks of passenger pigeons flew by they would darken the sky for days. There seemed to be no end to the huge flocks. Farmers were angry that the pigeons ate tiny plants in their grain fields so they killed as many as they could. Hunters killed millions of the birds each year and sold them in markets in the cities. By the time the West was settled, there were no passenger pigeons left. Today they are extinct.

The bison, or buffalo, was another animal that nearly perished. When travelers in the first wagon trains saw herds of buffalo on the prairies they couldn't believe their eyes. There were thousands of the big dark animals. Herds would cover valleys as far as the eye could see. Native North Americans hunted them for food and skins but travelers shot them just to see them fall. When the beaver skin trade ended, a lot of mountain men and trappers became buffalo hunters. They took wagons onto the prairies and shot thousands of buffalo, leaving the carcasses to rot while they took the hides away for sale. Later, after the meat had rotted away, bone hunters came with wagons and hauled the buffalo bones to cities, where the huge piles were ground up and used to make fertilizer and bone china. By 1882 there were only two hundred buffalo left on the plains. The Indians starved without a food source, and farm dwellers on the treeless prairie missed the buffalo chips they had burned for fuel. The days of the huge roaming herds were over.

If you want to see herds of buffalo today, check out the National Bison Range at Moiese, Montana. There are more than four hundred animals in the herd there. Yellowstone National Park in Wyoming is also the home to several hundred of the unusual animals. Buffalo are also being raised on ranches for meat. Sometimes you can buy buffalo burgers or steaks in restaurants or grocery stores in the West.

Rag Rug

Because it was so difficult to buy new items, and because people often didn't have much money, homesteaders tried to recycle everything. Even the dishwater and bathwater were saved to use in the garden. (After all, it had to be packed or pumped, and that was a lot of work!) Scraps from old clothing and fabric scraps were saved. Women and girls made these into quilts and rag rugs.

Here's a simple way to make a rug for your bedroom, using strips of old (or new) fabric.

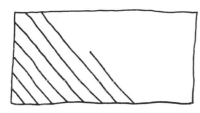

Cut the fabric strips on a slant.

Glue or sew the fabric strips together.

Make a slip knot around the crochet hook.

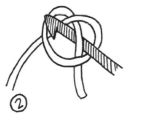

②

③

Pull it tight.

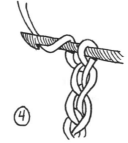

④

Make a chain stitch by pulling the rag through the loop on the hook. Make 30 chain stitches.

Materials

Woven broadcloth or calico fabric (bright-colored bedsheets can be used, too)

Scissors

Needle and thread or fabric glue

Crochet hook, the largest size you can find (Size K)

Cut the fabric into strips 1 inch wide and as long as possible. Cut the strips in a slanting direction (this is known as *cutting on the bias* of the fabric). This makes the strips less likely to ravel. When you have at least 20 strips cut, join them together at the ends to make 1 long strip. Sew or glue (use fabric glue) the ends together. Roll the long strip into a big ball, so it's easier to work with. Cut and glue more strips as you need them.

Using the last fabric strip, make a slip knot. Make a loop with the fabric strip, push the hook through it and pull it tight so it fits around the hook. Now you're ready to crochet.

Make a *chain stitch* first. Wrap the strip over the hook like the drawing. Pull the fabric strip through the loop that's on the hook to make a new loop. Don't pull the loops tight. That's 1 chain stitch. Make 30 chain stitches just like the first one.

Now it's time to do *single-crochet* stitches. Push the hook into the first chain stitch next to the hook. Wrap the strip over the hook, and pull the strip through the first loop only. Wrap the strip over the hook again, and pull it through both loops on the hook. This makes 1 single-crochet stitch.

Keep crocheting, working 1 single-crochet stitch in each stitch of the chain. When you get to the end of the chain, flip your work over and make another row of crochet stitches, working 1 in each loop of the last row. Keep crocheting, row by row, to make a rug 24 inches (2 feet) long, or as long as you wish. Tie the last stitch into a knot and tuck the end of the fabric strip under a few stitches to hide it.

When the rug gets dirty, flip it over to the other side, or wash it in a washing machine.

Pull through both loops leaving only 1 loop on the hook.

Pull through the first loop only. Loop the yarn over again.

Loop over the hook.

In a hurry? Here's a quick project that's not as big as a rug. Make a hot pad for the kitchen by making a chain 20 stitches long and working rows of crochet to make a piece 12 inches long.

To make a single-crochet stitch, put the hook through the loop next to the stitch on the hook. Wrap the rag over the hook and pull it through the first loop only. Now you have 2 loops on the hook. Wrap the rag around the hook again and this time, pull it through both of the loops on the hook. You've made 1 single crochet stitch. Keep going, turning the work at the end of each row and repeating row by row.

Good Times

Life was hard for homesteaders, but they found ways to have a lot of fun, too. Work and tasks that needed to be done were shared and turned into a chance for a party. Corn husking parties, barn buildings, and haying parties were chances for neighbors to gather, get the work done, and enjoy themselves at the same time. Dancing was popular, and when Saturday night came, people dressed up in their best clothing and rode to the church hall, schoolhouse, or neighbor's barn for a dance. Western dancers loved doing square dances. At a square dance, everyone had a partner but young and old people could all dance at the same time. Babies, grand-parents, brothers, and sisters—everyone enjoyed some homemade punch, goodies, and having fun.

To get ready for the dance, people took a bath (usually they only bathed once a week!), washed and ironed their best clothing, and polished their good shoes. Shoes could be polished with bear grease or the greasy black soot from inside the stove. Boys rubbed a bit of butter into their hair. Girls didn't wear makeup; instead they used a flannel cloth to dab talcum powder on their face and they pinched their cheeks to make them pink. One pair of sisters had a single pair of dress-up shoes between them. They wore moccasins, and took turns wearing the shoes to dance in.

Rag Curls

Here's how girls on homesteads curled their long hair into gorgeous corkscrew curls for fancy occasions. It still works!

Materials

Cotton cloth or an old sheet

Comb

Water

It takes 2 people to do this, so take turns with a friend or sister. Tear the cloth into strips about 1 inch wide and 24 inches long. You'll need 1 long strip for each curl. Work with wet hair and a comb. The hairdresser divides the hair into sections and the girl holds 1 end of the strip at the top of her head, with about 6 inches extending. The hairdresser wraps the wet hair around the rag, winding it towards the bottom. Wrap the rag back around the curled hair, covering it completely to hold it in place. Wrap the curl toward the top end of the rag. Tie the ends of the rag together at the top of the curl. Keep the rags in place until the hair is dry, then gently unwind, brush out the curls, and shape them around your fingers.

The girl holds the top of the rag while the hairdresser wraps the wet hair around the rag. Wrap it tightly.

Hold the hair in place by wrapping the rag back over the hair. Knot the ends at the top.

When the hair dries it can be styled in long "sausage" curls.

Square Dance

Square dancing was called that because the dance took place in a square formation. Dancing in a square began in France, and became very popular in the American West. Every square dance needed a *caller*. A caller was a fellow with a loud voice who could call out the dance formations for the dancers and be heard during this lively dance. Dance music was played by a fiddler or an accordion player. It didn't take much to have a good time!

You'll need eight people to dance in each square. Pick a caller (the caller can be one of the dancers). Take plenty of time to practice, and go slowly at first. Once everyone knows the steps, turn on the music and speed it up! For music, try to get a recording of lively square dancing music—a favorite song is "Turkey in the Straw."

Square your set. Stand in a square formation beside your partner. Everybody faces into the center. (Note: The black feet show where the boys stand; the white, where the girls stand.)

Square your set. Everyone faces center.

Bow to your partner. Turn to face your partner and bow to them. Then turn back to the beginning position.

Bow to your partner. Everyone turns to their partner and bows.

Allemande left. Turn to the person beside you who isn't your partner, and hold their left hand with your left hand. Walk a full turn to the left. Turn back to your partner and drop hands.

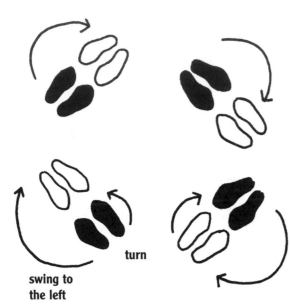

turn

swing to
the left

**Allemande left. Turn to the person beside you (not your partner) and, holding left hands, make a full turn to the left.
Drop hands and go back to face your partner.**

Grand right and left. Hold your partner's right hand with your right hand and walk by them. Put your left hand out to the next person in the square and walk by them. Keep going around the square switching from left to right hands as you walk by them, until you meet your partner again.

**Grand right and left.
Hold your partner's right hand with yours. Swing on past them to the next dancer. Hold left hands and dance on past to the next dancer, taking right hands. Keep going, right then left until you return to your partner.**

Swing your partner. Loop right arms at the elbows and swing each other around, staying in the same spot in the square. All four couples swing around once, at the same time.

Promenade back home. Partners link their arms, hands at the hip. The girl uses her left arm, the boy his right arm. Walk around the square a complete circle until you're both back where you started.

**Swing your partner
Stay in your spot in the square as you swing your partner around.**

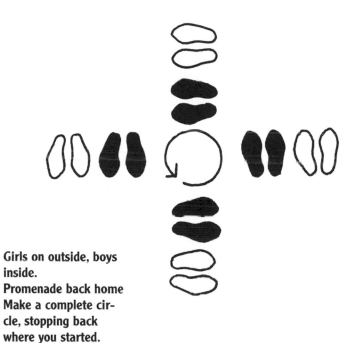

**Girls on outside, boys inside.
Promenade back home
Make a complete circle, stopping back where you started.**

Root Beer for a Crowd

There weren't many fancy drinks available in the West. Lemonade was the most popular, but lemons were only grown in warm climates. People tried to make up other drinks that tasted good, but sometimes simple cold water was the beverage—even at wedding receptions.

Root beer has been around a long time. People used to make it from the roots of the sarsaparilla plant, which grows in North America. Here's how to make enough for an entire classroom, birthday party, or family reunion.

Ingredients

Schilling Root Beer Concentrate (in spice/flavoring section of the grocery store)*

5 pounds sugar

5 gallons lukewarm water

½ package dry yeast, dissolved in 1 cup lukewarm water

Utensils

5 1-gallon plastic jugs with snap-on plastic lids or corks (wash with hot soapy water and rinse thoroughly)

5-gallon or larger plastic wastebasket or small plastic garbage can—use a new one, and save it just for making root beer (Don't use an aluminum container.)

Long-handled wooden or plastic stirring spoon

Plastic juice pitcher

Funnel

Put the sugar in the large plastic wastebasket. Pour in water and the root beer concentrate. Mix it well with the spoon. Stir the bottom of the container so the sugar dissolves. Dissolve the yeast in 1 cup of lukewarm water and stir it into the root beer mixture. Stir well.

When it's all dissolved and well mixed, fill the clean plastic jugs by dipping the juice pitcher into the root beer mixture and pouring it into the jugs. A funnel makes pouring easier. Fill each jug to within 1 inch of the top. Snap on the plastic cap. Place the filled jugs in a warm place for 1 or 2 days. (Room temperature is fine.) Bubbles will begin to form in the root beer as the yeast causes fermentation. This will make it fizzy. Chill the root beer before you serve it. Keep it in the refrigerator for 3 or 4 days if you don't drink it right away.

If you can't find root beer concentrate in your store, write to the McCormick Company, PO Box 208, Hunt Valley, MD 21030-0208.

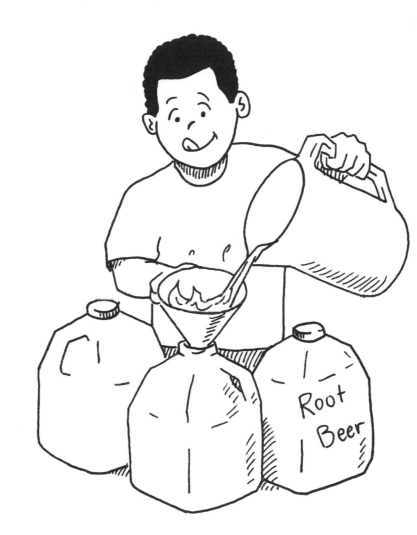

Popcorn Balls

Corn was one of the most easily grown crops in homesteaders' fields and gardens. Native North Americans had been growing it for a long time in their gardens when they introduced it to the European explorers. Within a short time, everyone in North America was eating something made from corn. Here's a tasty treat to make from popcorn, that would have been very popular at frontier parties. In those days it would have been made with molasses. Here's an easy way to do it.

Ingredients

60 bite-size caramel candies (unwrapped)

¼ cup water

1 gallon popped corn (about ½ cup before popping)

Mix caramels and water in a sauce pan.

Utensils

Saucepan

Spoon

Large bowl or roasting pan

Waxed paper

(Adult help suggested.)
Put the popcorn in the large bowl. Put the caramels and water in a saucepan. Heat on medium-low heat and stir continually. When the caramels are melted and the mixture is smooth pour it over all the popped corn. Wet your hands with water so the caramel won't stick to them and begin shaping the popcorn mixture into balls the size of baseballs. Set them on waxed paper. They will be firm in about 1 hour; sooner if you put them in the refrigerator to chill. This makes about 16 popcorn balls. If you want to store them, put each popcorn ball in a plastic sandwich bag.

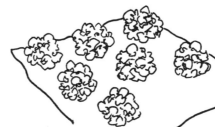

Shape the balls and set them on waxed paper.

When melted, pour the mixture over popped corn.

Mock Apple Pie

If fresh food wasn't available, pioneer cooks made do with what they had. Here's how to make apple pie—when you don't have any apples! It would have been a welcome dessert at a cabin building party given to welcome new homesteaders to the area.

Ingredients

2 pastry crusts for 9-inch pies

36 round cheese-flavored crackers (like Ritz)

1½ cups sugar

1½ cups water

1½ teaspoons cream of tartar

1 teaspoon grated lemon peel or orange peel

2 tablespoons lemon juice

2 tablespoons butter or margarine

Cinnamon, for sprinkling

Utensils

Pie pan

Saucepan

Spoon

Table knife

Cookie sheet

(Adult help suggested.)

Preheat the oven to 425° F.

Put the bottom pie crust in the pie pan. Break the crackers into quarters and put them in the crust.

Put the sugar, water, and cream of tartar in the saucepan. Stir. Bring the mixture to boiling. Simmer it on low for 15 minutes. Remove the saucepan from the heat. Stir in the lemon or orange peel and lemon juice (settlers would have probably used vinegar— our version will taste a bit better). Let the mixture cool in the saucepan. When it's cool, pour it over the crackers in the pie crust. Dab bits of butter on top of the crackers. Sprinkle cinnamon over the crackers, too.

Put the top crust on the pie. Pinch the edges together all around, to keep the juice from running out during baking. Use a table knife to cut a large "A"

in the center of the crust (or any letter or design you choose). These slits will let steam escape while the pie is cooking. Place the pie pan on a cookie sheet and put it in the oven. The cookie sheet will catch any juice that drips while baking, and keep the bottom of the oven clean.

Bake the pie at for about 35 minutes. Serve it while it's still warm. You can't tell it's not real apple pie!

Button, Button

Here's an old-time game that was played at parties or anytime people wanted to have fun with a simple guessing game. All you need is a button and several players.

Materials

1 button

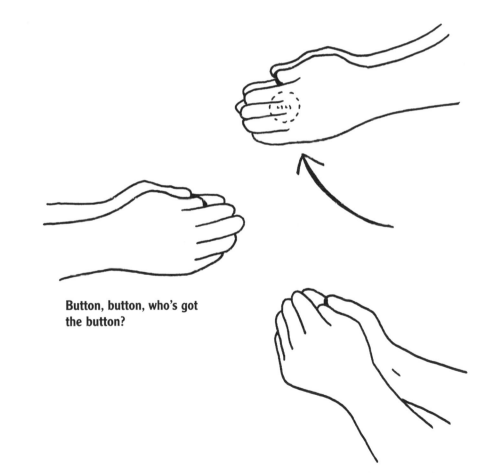

Button, button, who's got the button?

Everyone sits in a circle with their hands in their laps. Choose 1 person to be "It." "It" slips the button between their hands and holds their hands in a praying position, palms together, fingers straight. All the other players put their hands together with fingers straight, too. They hold their hands in position in front of them during the entire game.

The one who is "It" slips their hands between each of the players' hands, moving slowly and 1 at a time. As they pass their hands between all the players' hands, they secretly let the button slip out of their hands into 1 of the player's hands. Then they keep on passing their hands through the rest of the players', pretending they still have the button. After "It" has passed their hands between all the other players' hands, take turns guessing who has the button. If someone guesses correctly, they become the next "It." The tricky part is for the person who had the button passed secretly into their hands to try to keep from accidentally showing it by the look on his or her face.

Ridin' the Range

The era of the cowboys and cattle drives across the western plains and prairies began after the Civil War. Many people moved to the West after the war. Settlers living in the West were in the market to buy beef. Army troops needed beef and railroad workers building rail lines across the country needed to be fed. The Native North Americans who were put on reservations had no animals to hunt and were starving. The U.S. government needed to purchase cattle to supply the Indians as they had promised in treaties.

And there were so many cattle! There were five or six million wild cattle roaming around the area that is now Texas. These cattle were originally from Spain, brought to the New World on Spanish ships beginning in 1519. Mexican ranchers raised huge herds of cattle, but there was no market to sell the cattle to. Mexican cities were too far away. Some cattle wandered off the huge ranches, others were stolen. Eventually there were so many running wild that a rancher had only to round them up to stock a new ranch. But they were still too far away from a market to sell them.

The cattle weren't very valuable in Texas, because there was no one to sell them to. A steer in Texas country was worth about four dollars. Up north, it would sell for forty dollars—ten times the amount! It seemed that all a cowboy needed to do was head south, round up a herd of the wild critters, and drive them north to a railroad loading center, army fort, or town. It *sounded* simple enough.

Actually a cattle drive was complicated and well planned. It had to be in order to get three thousand wild cattle to go where a cowboy wanted them to.

A cattle drive was directed by a *trail boss*. He was in charge of everyone and everything—men, horses, and cattle. There was one cowboy for about every three hundred cattle. The second-in-charge was called the *straw boss* or *segundo* (that means *second* in Spanish). There was a cook, who was in charge of the *chuck wagon*, a large wagon that held all the food, medicines, and firewood for cooking fires. A *remuda man* was in charge of the extra horses. Each cowboy had from five to nine horses in the *remuda*, or horse herd, so he would have a fresh horse when he needed it.

When the herd started moving, everyone took their assigned place. *Point men* rode up front, on each side of the herd, so the cattle would know where to go. *Flank riders* rode along beside the moving herd. Men who rode *drag* rode at the back, in the thick dust behind the moving herd. They watched for stragglers and kept the animals moving. It was the worst spot to ride, so usually new recruits or young boys rode drag. A scout was sent about a day ahead of the herd to look for drinking water and safe places to cross rivers.

Cattle are interesting animals. When a herd first begins to move, several animals will try to be leader. They crowd and push to be at the front. Eventually the leaders earn their places at the front, and all the other animals fall in place behind them. After a few days, the animals all know their usual spot in the moving herd. Even after being mixed up at night, or after a storm or stampede, they will all go to their usual spots in the herd once it gets moving again.

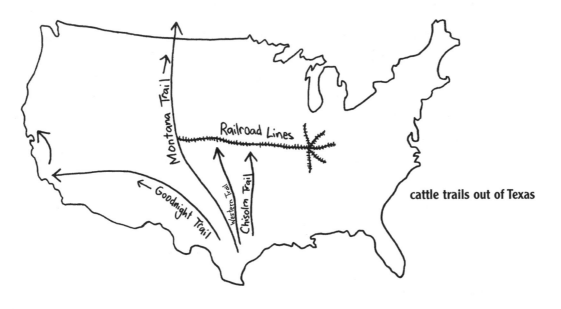

cattle trails out of Texas

Saddle Songs

At night the cattle lay down and slept while the cowboys kept watch. Because almost anything will spook cattle and cause them to stampede, they had to watch for wandering herds of buffalo, bands of unfriendly North American Indians, cattle rustlers, storms, and prairie fires. To keep the cattle contented at night and to keep themselves from getting too lonesome, cowboys on night watch sang as they rode around the herd. Cowboys sang together around the campfire, too, for fun and to keep from getting bored. Some say that a trail boss simply wouldn't hire a cowboy who couldn't sing.

Here's a simple cowboy saddle song from long ago. You can make up your own tune to go with the words:

My home is my saddle,

My roof is the sky;

The prairies I'll ride

Till the day that I die.

Perhaps you've sung "Home on the Range." It's one of the most popular songs handed down to us from the cowboy days.

Home on the Range

VERSE 1:

Oh, give me a home where the buffalo roam,

Where the deer and the antelope play;

Where seldom is heard a discouraging word,

And the skies are not cloudy all day.

CHORUS:

Home, home on the range;

Where the deer and the antelope play;

Where seldom is heard a discouraging word,

And the skies are not cloudy all day.

VERSE 2:

Where the air is so pure, the zephyrs so free,

The breezes so balmy and light,

That I would not exchange my home on the range,

For all the cities so bright.

CHORUS (REPEAT)

VERSE 3:

How often at night when the heavens are bright

With the light of the glittering stars,

Have I stood here amazed and asked as I gazed

If their glory exceeds that of ours.

CHORUS (REPEAT)

VERSE 4:

Oh, I love these wild flowers in this dear land of ours;

The curlew I love to hear scream;

And I love the white rocks and the antelope flocks

That graze on the mountain-tops green.

Chorus (repeat)

VERSE 5:

Oh, give me a land where the bright diamond sand

Flows leisurely down the stream;

Where the graceful white swan goes gliding along

Like a maid in a heavenly dream.

CHORUS (REPEAT)

VERSE 6:

Then I would not exchange my home on the range,

Where the deer and the antelope play;

Where seldom is heard a discouraging word,

And the skies are not cloudy all day.

(FROM GREAT AMERICAN FOLKLORE, COMPILED BY KEMP P. BATTLE)

Here's another:

I Am a Texas Cowboy

Oh, I am a Texas cowboy, right off the Texas plains,

My trade is cinchin' saddles, and pullin' bridle reins;

And I can throw a lasso with the greatest of ease;

I can rope and ride a bronco any way I please.

And when we get 'em, bedded down and settled for the night,

Some Cayuse shakes his saddle and he gives the herd a fright.

And as they madly stampede and gallop fast away,

In the heat of the moment I can hear some cowboy say:

Oh, I am a Texas cowboy, just off the stormy plains.

My trade is horses, cinches, saddles, ropes, and bridle reins.

Oh, I can tip a lariat and with a graceful ease

I can rope a streak of lightnin' and I ride it where I please.

Again we got 'em bedded down; I'm feelin' most forlorn.

A fire in the west arises and with lightnin' on their horns.

The boss says, "Boys, yore pay is here, you'll get it all in gold."

Oh, I'm bound to follow the longhorns until I am too old.

(FROM A TREASURY OF WESTERN FOLKLORE, BY B. A. BOTKIN)

Cowboy songs are really rhyming poems, sung to a musical tune. Today there are many people writing poetry about the West. The cowboy poetry gatherings in western states are fun to attend. Maybe you would like to try making up some cowboy poetry, to recite at one of the gatherings? The biggest is held every year in Elko, Nevada.

Cattle Drive Game

A cattle drive encountered a number of challenges along the way. As the herd moved north, the *outfit* (or group) might be charged a toll to cross Indian Territory (now Oklahoma). The toll would range from ten cents to one dollar per animal, to allow the cattle to cross the tribal lands. When the outfit got to Kansas, the cowboys had to beware of marauding bands of murdering thieves. The herd would also meet with angry farmers who tried to keep the wild longhorn cattle away from their fields. The wild longhorns carried a virus which would often kill other breeds of cattle. Other hazards they might meet up with were raging rivers, quicksand in river crossings, alkali water, poison weeds that drove the cattle insane, and prairie fires. By the time the outfit got to the end of the trail, they were all ready to call it quits—until the next season.

Make up your own game so you and friends can play the parts of cowboys on the trail.

Materials
Card stock or construction paper
Scissors
Pencil, pen, or markers
1 pound dry beans

Cut the card stock or construction paper into card-sized rectangles. Make them all the same size. You'll want to make at least 20 cards per player. Keep some cards blank and add new cards to the deck as you think of them.

On each of the cards, write something that could happen on a trail drive. If it's a disaster or hazard, like a stampede or prairie fire, write down

Make up the set of cards.

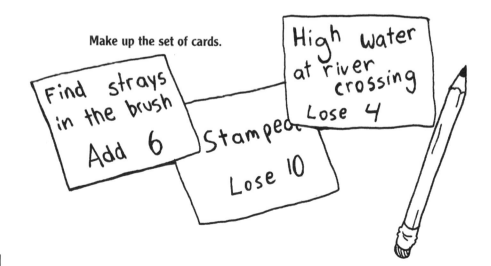

Large outfits had a calf wagon which was driven behind the herd to pick up newborn calves which could slow the herd down.

121

how many points a cowboy will lose. Keep the points on the cards under 10. Then make some cards that tell about good things that could happen, such as: a cow has a calf—"add 1 point." When all the cards are made, some with hazards, others with good things, shuffle them together and stack them face down on the table in front of the players. If you run out of ideas, you can make some cards alike, just be sure they aren't next to each other in the stack.

To play, give each player 50 dry beans. Put the leftover beans in a bowl in the center. The beans represent each player's herd of cattle. Take turns, each player drawing a card and either losing or adding beans to their own pile from those in the center bowl, following the directions on the cards. When all the cards are gone, count up beans to see who has the most cattle left.

Here are some ideas to put on cards:
Quicksand at river crossing—lose 7
Thieves stampede the herd—lose 9
Strays wander into camp—add 8
Horse breaks a leg—lose 6
Rattlesnake!—lose 2
Fair weather ahead—add 4
Pay the toll—lose 5
No water for miles—lose 4
Low water at river crossing—add 2
You fall asleep on night watch—lose 9
Lead cow has twin calves—add 2

Cowboys sometimes kept wallow-stones in their mouths during the long dusty ride. A wallow-stone was a round pebble, about the size of a pea, which a cowboy held in his mouth when he was thirsty. A wallow-stone in the mouth helped saliva keep a dry mouth and throat moist.

Draw from the stack of cards. Follow the directions on the card to add beans to or subtract beans from your pile using the extra beans in the bowl.

What's a Cowboy?

Which is which? Cowboy, cowhand, cowpuncher—all three were terms that meant something different. The term *cowboy* was first used in the Texas country to identify cattle rustlers who came down into the Mexican ranches and stole cattle to drive north. It was later used to mean anyone who worked on trail drives. A *cowhand* was used to identify someone who worked on a ranch. A *cowpuncher* was the term used for those who rode along with cattle on railroad cattle cars. They kept long poles to poke between the bars of the cattle car to keep the animals from lying down. A downed animal in a crowded railroad car was likely to get injured or be killed by the other cattle. Many of the cowboys did take jobs as punchers on the trains when they reached the rail line. Riding the *rattlers* (trains) to the nearest big town gave them a chance to see some excitement and spend their money.

Cowboys were also called *buckaroos*, which was a term that came from the Mexican cattlemen in early California. It came from mispronouncing the Spanish word for cowboy, *vaquero* (say it: back-air-oh). Vaqueros were highly skilled horsemen. They hated to get off the horse to do any of the ranch work with the cattle, so they became experts with ropes. They could rope calves, drag them to the branding fire, and even do the branding from horseback.

What did cowboys wear? Probably not exactly what you think. They didn't wear Levi's, the jeans that are so popular now. Levi's were made for miners, who needed the metal rivets to hold pockets together that were stuffed with rocks and minerals. Cowboys wore long trousers, knee-high boots, and long-sleeved shirts. The high boots kept their pants from getting torn on brush and brambles, and the long sleeves on the shirts protected their arms from the sun and wind.

Cowboy boots were very important. They were a cowboy's pride and joy, as well as safety equipment for the job. The high, under cut heels kept the foot from slipping through the stirrup if the rider was thrown from the horse. Being thrown or dragged with a foot caught in a stirrup could mean a broken leg or worse injuries. The loose boot top was made so a cowboy could pull his foot out of the boot quickly if he got hung up in the stirrup. A tight, laced boot wouldn't come off. If a cowboy is roping while standing, the high narrow heels dig into the ground and give him a better footing while he manages a struggling calf on the other end of the rope. The pointed toes of cowboy boots make it easier to get a foot into the stirrup quickly, especially if a horse is acting up. The high boot tops protect the legs from mesquite thorns, brush, and even snakes. Even the fancy stitching had a purpose—it stiffens the leather of the boot so it stands straight up and doesn't flop. Cowboy boots aren't made for walking, however.

Spurs were worn by the early Spanish conquistadors and have always been part of a western rider's equipment. A spur is a metal heel band with a pointed metal wheel that is fastened to a cowboy's boot heel. The blunt points are used to jab into the side of a horse that is misbehaving. Cowboys used to enjoy the sound of their spurs hitting the floor as they walked in town, and many wore spurs with *rowels* (the wheel part) that were six inches or more in diameter. Spurs were often decorated with a lot of fancy metalwork and made of silver.

Every cowboy wore a *bandanna*. It was just about the most useful piece of equipment a cowboy owned. A bandanna was a large handkerchief, usually red printed cotton. Cowboys wouldn't wear white ones, because they reflected light and could be seen at a distance and might spook cattle. White also got too dirty. The bandanna was usually worn folded in half diagonally, and tied in a knot around the neck. The knot was worn in the back and the bandanna hung loosely at the neck. That way it could be pulled up over the nose and

mouth when riding in the dust behind cattle. It would protect the face from harsh wind, too. In the morning, a cowboy could use a bandanna to wash his face. If he needed a blindfold for a nervous horse, he could use his bandanna, tied over the horse's eyes. A bandanna was useful to wipe away sweat, as a hot pad to protect his hand when holding a hot branding iron, and to bind up wounds. In a fierce wind, a bandanna could tie a hat to the cowboy's head. It could be used as a flag to signal across the plains to someone else. Large, flowing neckerchiefs held in place with a slide or fastener didn't come into fashion until later when movie cowboys and dude ranches started to appear.

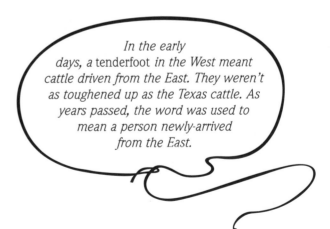

In the early days, a tenderfoot *in the West meant cattle driven from the East. They weren't as toughened up as the Texas cattle. As years passed, the word was used to mean a person newly-arrived from the East.*

Serape

Cowboys wore vests because there were no short coats sold in those days. Long coats were used as raincoats and were useful because they could be draped over the saddle to keep it dry during storms. In Texas and Arizona the *serape* (say it: suh-raw-pay) was popular among both rich and poor people. It began in the Southwest and Mexico, where women wove colorful wool blankets into bright patterns. It could be slipped over the head easily, and kept arms free for riding and roping. When a serape wasn't needed, it could be rolled up and tied on behind the saddle. At night it made a soft pillow for sleeping on the hard ground.

Materials

2 bath towels

Straight pins

Needle and thread, or sewing machine

Scissors

Fringe, if desired

Lay the 2 towels side by side on a table. Pin them together down the center, leaving an opening in the middle large enough for you to slip your head through easily—about 18 inches. Slip it over your head while it's pinned to be sure it will fit easily. Then sew the towels together by hand or machine. If the towels have fringed ends, leave them as they are. If you want to add fringe, sew or glue it along the bottom edge of the front and back of the serape.

Sew 2 towels together, leaving an opening in the center for your head.

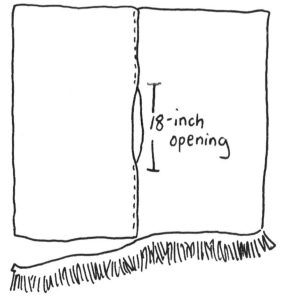

18-inch opening

Sew fringe on the bottom edges.

Cowboy Hats

Another important item of clothing was a cowboy's hat. The Mexican cowboys wore wide-brimmed *sombreros*, decorated with gold and silver embroidery thread. Other cowboys wore whatever they could find, until a teenager made a trip to Colorado. His name was John Stetson, and he made his own hat to wear as protection from the rain, snow, and sun of the Plains country. His first hat was made with crude tools, including a hatchet. He scraped the underfur from a dried rabbit hide, moistened it, and formed the material into a felt to make a large felt hat. It was an old-time method of making a hat. When he wore his large hat, everyone laughed and made jokes about it. He didn't laugh though, because when he was ready to return East from his trip he sold the hat for five dollars to a bull-whacker. The mule-team driver had paid a week's wages for his creation.

When John Stetson returned home to Philadelphia, he began making more hats. He called his hat the "Boss of the Plains." Within a few years, every cowboy wore one. By the time he died, John Stetson had made his idea into a large company, had sold thousands of western hats, and his name was used to describe a cowboy's hat: a Stetson.

A cowboy's hat was used in many ways. The wide brim kept the sun and rain off his face and neck. The hat could be used to fan a campfire into flame, to carry oats to a horse, as a pillow on the hard ground, and even for drinking water. A good hat was important, and a cowboy paid from two to six months of wages for one. Most cowboy hats were soft, smooth felt, in a light gray or light brown color. Some were black. The soft felt could be shaped to fit a cowboy's head.

Cowboys dented the crown and brim differently depending upon where they were from. The style in the Southwest was to leave the crown high, with three or four dents in the sides. In the Northwest, the crown was pushed flat on top, but had a pleat in it which made it lower.

Cowboys also put on their own hatbands, made from woven horsehair, stamped leather, or snakeskin. The hatband was a decoration, and could also tighten the hat to fit the wearer's head.

What About Cowgirls?

Women and girls learned to do much of the cattle work on their family's ranch, but few worked on other ranches or on cattle drives. Some girls did dress up as boys and got jobs on cattle drives, though, and the trail boss never knew he had hired girls.

In the 1800s most women and girls rode horseback on a sidesaddle. It was unladylike to ride astride in a man's saddle. That changed quickly in the West, where women made their own split skirts—sort of long culottes—for riding. Some girls made denim bloomers to wear under shorter denim skirts.

There weren't many cowgirls, but many girls became expert riders. Some could stand on top of a galloping horse, or do gymnastic routines at full speed, clinging to the saddle with one hand or foot. These trick riders became stars of the Wild West shows. Some girls even rode trained diving horses that leaped from high platforms into tanks of water for thrilled audiences.

Braided Leather Belt

Leather braiding has been done by horsemen since the days when the ancient Phoenicians taught braiding to the Moors of northern Africa in 1600 B.C. The Moors took the craft into Spain, and centuries later the Spanish horsemen brought the skill to the New World with the first horses in Mexico. Western cowboys learned how to braid from Mexicans in early California and Texas. A cowboy had to be able to braid leather in order to make his own *quirts* (a short-handled whip), bridles, reins, and other horse gear.

In order to braid leather, you need to cut a thong (a long narrow strip of leather) from a scrap. Here's how: Cut a circular shape, rounding the edges of a scrap to make it as large a piece of leather as you can, but with round edges. Start cutting the thong as wide as you want along the outer edge. Continue cutting in a spiral until you reach the center and run out of leather. Pull the thong to stretch it so it lies smooth.

Braid leather to make a belt you can wear.

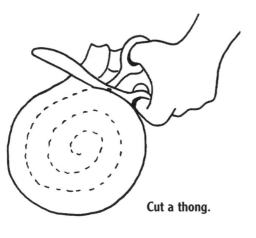

Cut 2 slits in the belt. Stop cutting 2 inches from one end.

Cut a thong.

Materials

Chamois (purchase from auto supply section of supermarket)

Scissors

Tape measure

D-ring belt buckle (found in fabric stores)

Super Glue

Measure your waistline, and add 8 inches. That's how long your belt will have to be. Cut a thong from the chamois, 2 inches wide and as long as you need for the belt.

Cut 2 slits lengthwise in the belt, but be sure you don't cut completely through one end of it. Leave about 2 inches uncut on one end. That will be where you fasten the buckle.

Slip the uncut end of the belt around a D-ring and use Super Glue to fasten the ends. Let it dry. Then insert the buckle end into a dresser drawer and gently close it over the belt—this will hold the end for you as you braid.

Braid the belt, overlapping the strips of leather according to the following pattern: bring the right-hand strip toward the center and over the middle strip. Next, take the left-hand strip and cross it over the middle strip. Repeat this pattern with the right strip and then the left in an alternating fashion until the entire belt is braided. Lay a strip of chamois (about 1 inch wide) over the braided strips at the end of the belt. This will help keep the belt from unraveling. Glue this small strip in place. Let the glue dry completely. To wear the belt, lace it through your trouser belt loops with the buckle in front. To fasten, slide the finished end inside the "D" of the buckle, then lace the end back the other direction, between the rings of the buckle. Pull the end to tighten.

Fold the end over the buckle and glue.

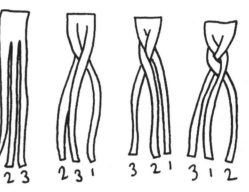

Braid the belt following this pattern.

1 2 3   2 3 1   3 2 1   3 1 2

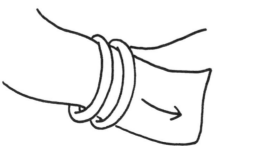

Glue a strip of leather across the ends to hold them.

To fasten the buckle, pull the belt through both rings. Then pull it back between them.

Braided Hatband or Bracelet

Here's how to make a braided leather hatband or bracelet.

Braid following this pattern.

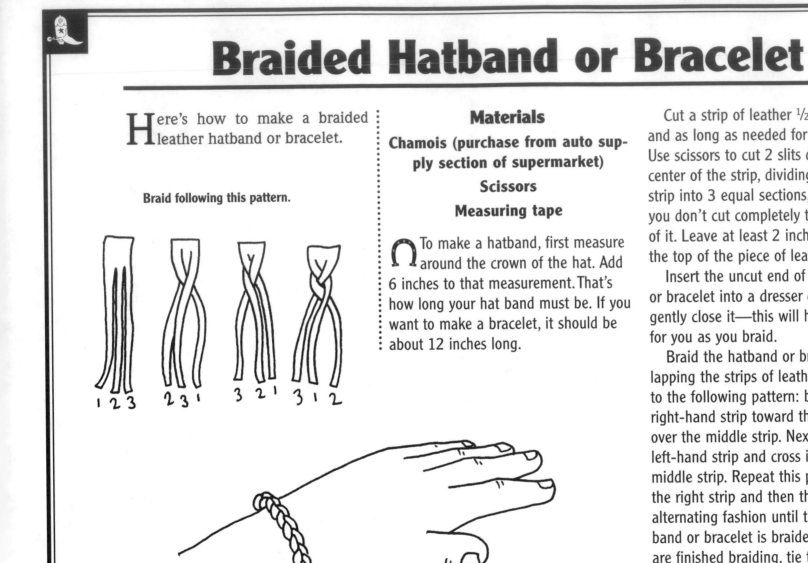

Materials

Chamois (purchase from auto supply section of supermarket)

Scissors

Measuring tape

To make a hatband, first measure around the crown of the hat. Add 6 inches to that measurement. That's how long your hat band must be. If you want to make a bracelet, it should be about 12 inches long.

Cut a strip of leather ½-inch wide and as long as needed for the project. Use scissors to cut 2 slits down the center of the strip, dividing the leather strip into 3 equal sections, but be sure you don't cut completely through 1 end of it. Leave at least 2 inches uncut at the top of the piece of leather.

Insert the uncut end of the hatband or bracelet into a dresser drawer and gently close it—this will hold the end for you as you braid.

Braid the hatband or bracelet, overlapping the strips of leather according to the following pattern: bring the right-hand strip toward the center and over the middle strip. Next, take the left-hand strip and cross it over the middle strip. Repeat this pattern with the right strip and then the left in an alternating fashion until the entire band or bracelet is braided. When you are finished braiding, tie the end in a knot. Place the braided band on your hat and tie it off or have someone tie the bracelet on your wrist.

Leather Stamped Bookmark

Cowboys loved fancy leather work on saddles, cuffs, belts, boots, and other gear. One way to decorate leather with interesting designs is by stamping it. Saddle stamping was an ancient craft used by the Moors in North Africa. Spanish conquistadors brought it to the American West, along with horses.

Leather stamps are metal tools with a design carved into them. The stamp is pressed into the leather by striking it with a heavy stick or mallet. Pretty flowers, leaves, letters, and basket weaving or other designs can be tinted with paint or stain when the work is finished. Cowboys sometimes made their own stamps by filing down the heads of large nails. Here's how you can try stamping some leather and make a bookmark.

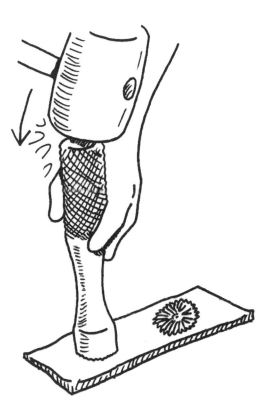

Using leather stamping tools, hammer a design into damp leather.

Materials

Heavy leather, also called tooling leather (sold in craft shops and leather supply stores)

Scissors

Washcloth

Hammer

Leather craft stamping tools*

(Adult help suggested.)

Cut the leather to the size you want. First, practice on a few scraps of leather to be sure you like the effects you get with the different stamping tools.

Wet the washcloth with water and wring it out. Use it to dampen both sides of the leather. Work on a firm surface, like a countertop. Use the hammer to firmly tap the end of the screwdriver or head of the nail into the damp leather, testing the mark it makes. A regular screwdriver makes a dash, which can be made into a straight line or zig zag. The Phillips screwdriver will make a tiny star or flower design. See what other things you can find that can be used.

After you have practiced with different items, decide on a design for the bookmark. Draw it on a piece of paper if you like. Then, following your design plan, go ahead and tap the design onto the dampened piece of leather for your bookmark. You can use markers to color in parts of the design. Leather dyes can also be used; they are sold at leather craft stores. Leather craft supplies are sold in most craft and hobby stores, or look in the Yellow Pages under "Leather."

You can buy these in leather craft stores, hobby shops, or substitute some of the following: screwdriver, Phillips screwdriver, large nail, assorted sized nuts and bolts, and any other small items that might leave an interesting mark on the leather. Or, you can write to the Tandy Leather Company, at 1400 Everman Parkway, Fort Worth, TX 76140, for a catalog of leather working kits and supplies.

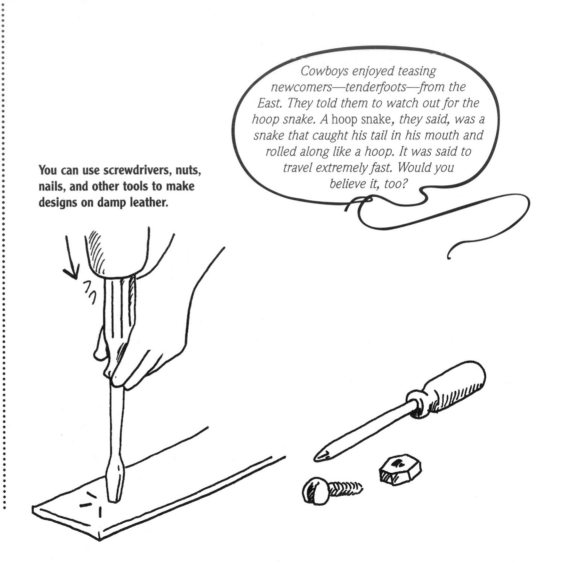

You can use screwdrivers, nuts, nails, and other tools to make designs on damp leather.

Cowboys enjoyed teasing newcomers—tenderfoots—from the East. They told them to watch out for the hoop snake. A hoop snake, they said, was a snake that caught his tail in his mouth and rolled along like a hoop. It was said to travel extremely fast. Would you believe it, too?

Poke Sack

Cowboys carried their money, gold, or other valuables in a little sack they called a *poke*. Pokes could be plain or fancy. Some were made by Native North American women and were decorated with lavish beadwork, embroidery, and fringe. Here's how to make a plain one; go ahead and trim or decorate it if you like.

Materials

2 6-by-8-inch pieces of fabric, felt, or chamois

Scissors

Ruler

Straight pins

Needle and thread or sewing machine

2 12-inch long pieces of cord or lacing

Small safety pin

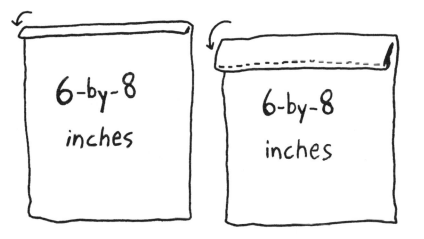

Turn the top edge under ¼ inch, then again ½ inch. Stitch. This is called the casing.

Cut 2 rectangles, each 6 inches by 8 inches. Turn the top edge down ¼ inch. Turn it under another ½ inch and stitch along the edge. Do the same on the other rectangle. This makes a casing for the cord to go through.

Pin the 2 rectangles together, with casing on the outside. Sew the sides together, going down one side, across the bottom, and up the other side. Begin and end the stitching below the casing on both sides. Turn the poke right side out.

Fasten the safety pin to one end of a piece of cord, and push the pin through the casing. It will pull the cord along through the casing. When both cords are pulled through the casing, knot the ends so they won't ravel.

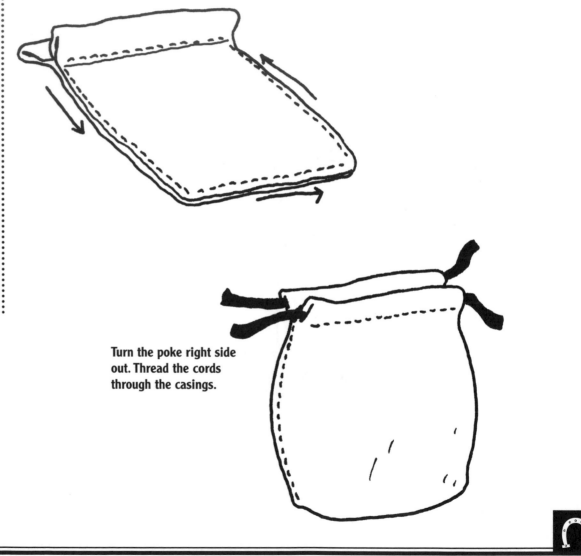

Stitch down 1 side, across the bottom, and up the other side. Start and stop stitching at the casing.

Turn the poke right side out. Thread the cords through the casings.

Knot Tying

Cowboys needed to be able to tie all kinds of knots—for tying up horses or cows, for tying loads onto pack saddles, and to secure gear. During rainy weather or winter, cowboys spent time in the *bunkhouse* (where all the cowboys slept) tying knots in order to perfect their skills. Some cowboys were experts at knot tying. They kept their methods for tying the hardest knots a secret and charged the others for lessons. If a cowboy knew how to tie a *fiador* knot, the hardest of all, he could charge from fifty to seventy-five cents just to tie one as a demonstration.

Here are some of the most useful and important knots:

Overhand knot: One end passes through a loop. This is the most basic knot, one you probably already use for everyday things.

Clove hitch knot: This knot uses two loops. It's useful to tie the end of a rope to a post. Practice on a fence or deck railing.

Honda knot: This is made up of two overhand knots. It makes an eye, or honda about two inches wide. It is used to make a noose for roping cattle.

Overhand knot

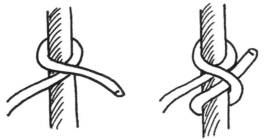

Clove hitch knot

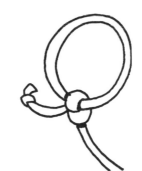

Honda knot

Neckerchief knot

Neckerchief knot: This is used to tie a bandanna around a cowboy's neck.

Hitching knot: This is useful to tie a horse up to a post, or a dog to a fence. Practice on a fence or deck railing.

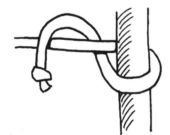
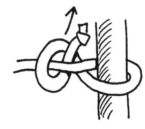

Hitching knot

Know Your Cans

While the cowboys idled away the long winter months, between building fences and cutting firewood, they played a game that sharpened their reading and memory skills. They would recite from memory the words on the labels of the canned foods that were used in the ranch house. Try it with some friends or your whole family. It's fun for readers of all ages.

Canned foods were popular in the West. The cowboys called them *airtights*. Peaches were the favorite, but canned tomatoes were popular in the desert because they were a good thirst quencher. Cowboys drank canned milk which they called *contented cow*. They would never stoop to milking a cow, unless it was a wild-cow milking contest in a rodeo.

Materials

3–4 different cans of food, one for each person; or front labels saved from several different cans of food

Kitchen timer

Index cards

Scissors

Paste or glue

To play, let each person pick the can they want to try. Set a timer for 3 minutes. During the 3 minutes, the players study the writing on their cans, trying to memorize every word—even punctuation! (That's how cowboys did it—of course back then cans didn't have nearly as much printed on them as cans do today.) When the time is up, each player gives her can to someone else, and tries to recite as much writing on the can as she can remember. (You may want to make the game easier by memorizing just the front of the can.)

Make the game a bit different by saving the front labels off of several different cans and gluing them to index cards. Pass the cards out, 1 to a player, set the timer for 3 minutes, then challenge everyone to recite what was on the label they were given. Mix the cards up and play another round, with everyone getting a different card.

Canned food became popular during the Civil War. It was invented by a Frenchman trying to win a prize from Napoleon for better ways to preserve food for France's army.

Blind Post Office

There were no post offices, telephones, or telegraph lines across most of the West. In order to pass messages to other cowboys, a *blind post office* was used. It was a special crevice in a rock or in a hole in the trunk of a tree, or some other hiding spot that was along the trail or range where the cowboys often passed. News items and letters could be tucked into the hiding spot to wait for the intended receiver to come along and pick them up. Outlaws and cattle rustlers used the same method for passing messages between themselves.

Look around your neighborhood for a hiding spot you and your friends can use. Plan it out ahead of time, and then begin using your secret spot to pass messages between yourselves.

Maybe your blind post office can be behind a loose brick. Leave messages for your friends to pick up.

Tally

Cowboys needed to be able to keep an accurate count of the number of cattle in their care. It was very important at branding time when cattle were being loaded onto railroad cars for shipment to market, or after a stampede on the trail. If the cattle were calm and standing around, the *tally man* kept a record with paper and pencil. At other times when the cattle were passing by or running up loading ramps, the tally man filled his pocket with small stones. As the cattle were driven past he would take a stone from the full pocket and put it in the empty pocket after each tenth cow. Or, he might cut notches on a stick, or tie knots in a string.

Try counting a tally of cars passing by or people walking past. Use pebbles, cut notches in a stick or strip of paper, or tie knots in a tally string.

Cowboys used the term vamoose to mean, "Let's go!" or "Get going!" It came from the Spanish word, vamos, which means "we go."

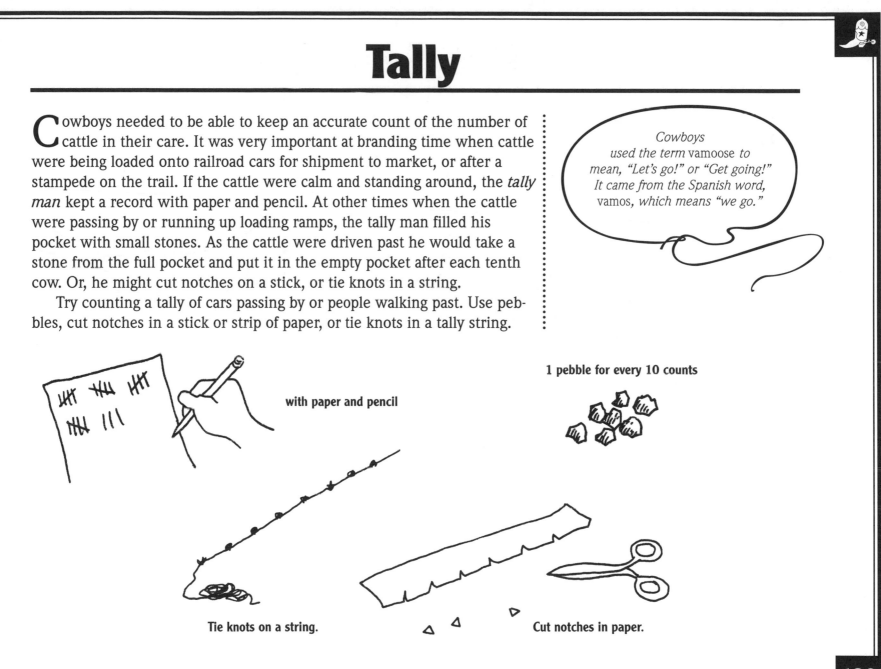

with paper and pencil

1 pebble for every 10 counts

Tie knots on a string.

Cut notches in paper.

Star Search

Night herders guarded the cattle herd at night. They would ride horseback around the sleeping herd in opposite directions. They usually sang or whistled a soft lullaby because it calmed the cattle. They didn't often have watches so they would tell time at night by using the stars. They would look for shapes made by stars, called *constellations*. The Big Dipper was an easy constellation to find. The stars of the Big Dipper swing around the North Star every twenty-four hours. Night herders going on duty would check where the Big Dipper was in relation to the North Star. When the movement of the stars had marked off a third of the night, the shift was over and two more cowboys were awakened to take the next shift as night herders. Night herders didn't work the entire night, as they needed some rest so they could do their regular work the next day.

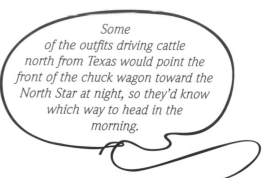

Some of the outfits driving cattle north from Texas would point the front of the chuck wagon toward the North Star at night, so they'd know which way to head in the morning.

3am

Midnight

6am

North Star (Polaris)

9pm

Chow Time!

Cowboys called their food *eats*, *chow*, and *grub*.
   What did cowboys eat? That depended on *Cookie*, or the cook. The cook drove the chuck wagon and fixed all the meals along the way. Trailside favorites were hot bread or biscuits, steak, beans, coffee, and the frontier favorite: Ambassador-brand yellow cling peaches, eaten in sweet syrup right out of the can. Cowboys liked their beef well done, and thought rare meat was unhealthy. *Mutton* (sheep) was never served to cowboys—they would never eat their hated competition for the range grass.

Before the Civil War only the wealthy and privileged drank coffee. Coffee beans were imported from Africa and South America, just like they are today. They were very expensive. During the Civil War, captured or donated stores of food were given to the soldiers with army rations. Coffee was enjoyed by thousands of men who tasted the brew for the first time during the war. After the war ended, and many of the soldiers and freed slaves went West, they took their taste for hot coffee with them. No cowboy went for long without a cup of coffee, usually with plenty of sugar and canned milk mixed in.

Chili con Carne

Beans were the main item in a cowboy's diet. They were easy to store, didn't need to be kept cold, were cheap, and Cookie couldn't do much to ruin them. Mexican cooks and cowboys shared this way of fixing beans, and it became a favorite of Westerners. *Chili* is the name of a pepper, *con* is Spanish for "with," and *carne* is Spanish for "meat." So, the name of this recipe is actually "chili with meat," but we usually include red beans, too.

Ingredients

½ pound ground beef

1 small onion, chopped

1 green pepper, chopped

1 16-ounce can tomatoes, broken up with a fork

1 16-ounce can dark red kidney beans

1 8-ounce can tomato sauce

1 teaspoon salt

1 teaspoon chili powder

Crackers or biscuits

Utensils

Large spoon

Skillet with a lid

(Adult help suggested.)

Cook the meat, chopped onion, and chopped pepper in the skillet until it is lightly browned. Stir in the tomatoes (don't drain off the juice), the can of beans, the tomato sauce, salt, and chili powder. Put on a lid and simmer at low heat for 1 hour. This makes enough to serve 4 people. Serve crackers or biscuits along with it.

Son-of-a-Gun Stew

This was a meal made up of all the odds and ends and leftovers the cook had on hand. When the cook made Son-of-a-Gun Stew, everybody hoped he was in a good mood—there was no telling what he would put in if he wasn't!

Here's how to make a simple stew. You can change it depending upon what's in your kitchen or refrigerator. You can use fresh, frozen, or canned vegetables.

Ingredients

3 carrots, chopped

3 celery stalks, chopped

2 or 3 potatoes, chopped

1 onion, chopped

1 small can tomatoes

1 15-ounce can ranch-style beans

6 bouillon cubes, beef or chicken

2 quarts water

1 teaspoon salt

Biscuits

Utensils

Large kettle

Stirring spoon

Kitchen knife

(Adult help suggested.)
Put the water, salt, and bouillon cubes in the kettle and bring the water to a boil over medium heat. Add the fresh vegetables, and simmer for 15 minutes. Add the tomatoes and beans. Simmer another 10 minutes. Serve with hot biscuits. Serves 4.

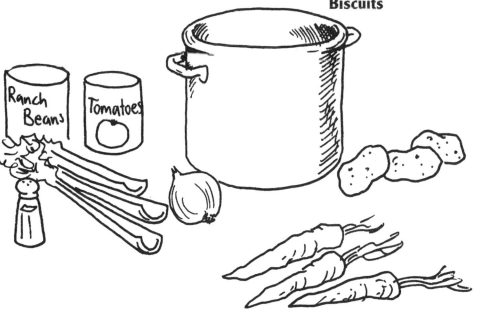

Here's an old joke about making cowboy coffee: Take 1 pound of coffee and wet it good with water. Boil it over a hot fire. Pitch a horseshoe in and if it sinks, put in some more coffee.

Cowboy Talk

Cowboys had particular ways to refer to cattle. Cattle were much more than *cows* (females) and *bulls* (males). To a cowboy, all cattle are born as *calves*. After a year, the male calf becomes a *bull* or *yearling*. The yearling becomes a *steer* on his second birthday. Two years later he is known as a *beef*. A female calf becomes a *heifer* on her first birthday. On her fourth birthday she becomes a *beef*. *Feeders* are cattle which are being fattened before selling, and *stockers* are those placed on the range. Cowboys usually call all cattle *cows* when talking about these animals.

Here are some cowboy phrases you might want to use in conversation sometime:

all horns and rattles—someone who is very angry

barkin' at a knot—wasting your time, trying to do something useless

doesn't use up all his kindlin' to make a fire—someone who doesn't waste words on small talk

mad as a peeled rattler—very angry

don't go wakin' snakes—don't make trouble

above my huckleberry—too hard for me to do

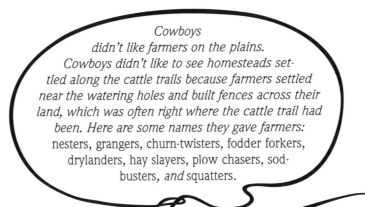

Cowboys didn't like farmers on the plains. Cowboys didn't like to see homesteads settled along the cattle trails because farmers settled near the watering holes and built fences across their land, which was often right where the cattle trail had been. Here are some names they gave farmers: nesters, grangers, churn-twisters, fodder forkers, drylanders, hay slayers, plow chasers, sod-busters, *and* squatters.

New Movement

The days of the cowboy and the open range didn't last long. The barbed wire fence was invented, and it soon stretched across the plains. So did the *Iron Horse*. That's what people called the railroad engines that pulled trains across the country. Railroad companies built tracks across the plains and prairies and brought thousands of settlers to the West. They sold them land alongside the railroad or brought them west with glowing newspaper advertisements printed in the East and Europe. By the end of the 1800s the days of the wide-open West were over. Most of it was settled by then, towns and villages had grown into cities, and life had become quite a bit like the places people had left behind.

Then a new movement began. In the 1890s, people living in the large cities on the Pacific coast—Seattle, Portland, and San Francisco—began moving toward the East! Settlers left these cities to find cheaper land, jobs, and better lives once again. They traveled eastward, settling states like Idaho, Nevada, and Arizona—from the West!

Bibliography

Bergon, Frank. *The Journals of Lewis and Clark*. New York: Penguin Books, 1989.

Blevins, Winfred. *Dictionary of the American West*. New York: Facts on File, 1993.

Botkin, B. A. *A Treasury of Western Folklore*. New York: Crown Publishers, 1951.

Foster-Harris, William. *The Look of the Old West*. New York: Viking Press, 1955.

Grant, Bruce. *The Cowboy Encyclopedia*. Chicago: Rand McNally, 1951.

Holmes, Kenneth L., ed. *Covered Wagon Women*. Spokane: Arthur H. Clark Company, 1994. Ten volumes.

Horan, James D. *The Great American West*. New York: Crown Publishers, 1978.

Karolevitz, Robert F. *Newspapering in the Old West*. New York: Bonanza Books, 1965.

Laycock, George, and Ellen Laycock. *How the Settlers Lived*. New York: David McKay Company, 1980.

Lee, C. Y. *Days of the Tong Wars: California 1847–1896*. New York: Ballantine Books, 1974.

Luchetti, Cathy. *Home on the Range: A Culinary History of the American West*. New York: Villard Books, 1993.

Marcy, Randolph B. *The Prairie Traveler*. New York: Berkley Publishing Company, 1994 reprint of 1859 edition.

Roach, Joyce Gibson. *The Cowgirls*. Denton, Texas: University of North Texas Press, 1990.

Sappington, Robert Lee. *The Lewis and Clark Expedition Among the Nez Perce Indians*. Moscow, Idaho: University of Idaho. Northwest Anthropological Research Notes, Spring, 1989.

Schlissel, Lillian. *Women's Diaries of the Westward Journey*. New York: Schocken Books, 1982.

Time-Life Books. *The Wild West*. New York: Warner Books, 1993.

Tunis, Edwin. *Frontier Living*. New York: Thomas Y. Crowell Company, 1961.

More books by LAURIE CARLSON from CHICAGO REVIEW PRESS

Classical Kids
An Activity Guide to Life in Ancient Greece and Rome
See what life was like in ancient Greece and Rome while having fun with hands-on activities such as making a star gazer, chiseling a clay tablet, weaving Roman sandals, and making a Greek mosaic.
ages 5–12
ISBN 1-55652-290-8
200 pages, paper, $14.95

Colonial Kids
An Activity Guide to Life in the New World
Young adventurers can learn about the settling of America while enjoying activities like stitching a sampler, pitching horseshoes, making an almanac, churning butter, and more.
"Colonial America comes to life in this attractive and easy-to-use book."
—*School Library Journal*
"The projects offer insight into the colonists' daily life."
—*Publishers Weekly*
ages 5–12
ISBN 1-55652-322-X
160 pages, paper, $12.95

Green Thumbs
A Kid's Activity Guide to Indoor and Outdoor Gardening
With a few seeds, some water and soil, and this book, kids will be creating gardens of their own in no time.
"Carlson is an expert at suggesting imaginative activities. Fun, as well as educational."
—*Skipping Stones*
ages 5–12
ISBN 1-55652-238-X
144 pages, paper, $12.95

Days of Knights and Damsels
An Activity Guide
"A project-stuffed activity guide to the Middle Ages."
—*Home Education Magazine*
"This book helps you experience the era of kings, queens, and castles with more than a hundred easy projects straight out of the Middle Ages."
—*FACES*
ages 5–12
ISBN 1-55652-291-6
184 pages, paper, $14.95

Kids Camp!
Activities for the Backyard or Wilderness
Laurie Carlson and Judith Dammel
Young campers will build an awareness of the environment, learn about insect and animal behavior, boost their self-esteem, and acquire all the basic skills for fun, successful camping.
"A good guide to outdoor adventures for inexperienced young campers and their families."
—*School Library Journal*
ages 5–12
ISBN 1-55652-237-1
184 pages, paper, $12.95

More Than Moccasins
A Kid's Activity Guide to Traditional North American Indian Life
Kids will discover traditions and skills handed down from the people who first settled this continent.
"As an educator who works with Indian children I highly recommend [*More Than Moccasins*] for all kids and teachers. . . . I learned things about our Indian world I did not know."
—*Bonnie Jo Hunt*
Wicahpi Win (Star Woman)
Standing Rock Lakota
ages 5–12
ISBN 1-55652-213-4
200 pages, paper, $12.95

Kids' Activity Books the Whole Family Can Enjoy

Best Friends
Tons of Crazy, Cool Things to Do with Your Girlfriends
Lisa Albregts and Elizabeth Cape
Fun activities to help friends grow closer, have a great time, and forge lifetime memories.
ISBN 1-55652-326-2
168 pages, paper, $12.95

Big Book of Fun
Creative Learning Activities for Home & School, Ages 4–12
Carolyn Buhai Haas
Illustrated by Jane Bennet Phillips
Includes more than 200 projects and activities—from indoor-outdoor games and nature crafts to holiday ideas, cooking fun, and much more.
ISBN 1-55652-020-4
280 pages, paper, $14.95

Frank Lloyd Wright for Kids
Kathleen Thorne-Thomsen
A thorough biography is followed by stimulating projects that enable kids to grasp the ideas underlying Wright's work—and have fun in the process.
ages 8 & up
ISBN 1-55652-207-X
144 pages, paper, $14.95

Leonardo da Vinci for Kids
His Life and Ideas
Janis Herbert
The marriage of art and science is celebrated in this beautifully illustrated four-color biography and activity book.
ages 8 & up
ISBN 1-55652-298-3
104 pages, paper, $16.95

Loaves of Fun
A History of Bread with Activities and Recipes from Around the World
Elizabeth M. Harbison
Illustrated by John Harbison
More than 30 recipes and activities take kids on a multicultural journey to discover bread and the people who created, cooked, ate, and enjoyed it.
ages 6–12
ISBN 1-55652-311-4
110 pages, paper, $12.95

Math Games & Activities from Around the World
Claudia Zaslavsky
More than 70 math games, puzzles, and projects from all over the world are included in this delightful book for kids who think math is boring.
ISBN 1-55652-287-8
160 pages, paper, $14.95

My Own Fun
Creative Learning Activities for Home and School
Carolyn Buhai Haas and Anita Cross Friedman
More than 160 creative learning projects and activities for elementary-school children.
ages 7–12
ISBN 1-55652-093-X
194 pages, paper, $9.95

On Stage
Theater Games and Activities for Kids
Lisa Bany-Winters
Have fun above the footlights while playing theater games, learning about puppetry and pantomime, making sound effects, costumes, props, and scenery, applying stage makeup; and more. Several play scripts are included.
ages 6–12
ISBN 1-55652-324-6
160 pages, paper, $14.95

Shaker Children
True Stories and Crafts
Kathleen Thorne-Thomsen
This charming book combines two true biographies and authentic activities to tell children of today about the Shakers of yesterday.
ages 8 & up
ISBN 1-55652-250-9
128 pages, paper, $15.95

Shakespeare for Kids
His Life and Times
Colleen Aagesen and Margie Blumberg
Kids can get their first taste of the Bard's sublime craft with this lively biography and activity book.
ages 8 & up
ISBN 1-55652-347-5
144 pages, paper, $14.95

Watch Me Grow
Fun Ways to Learn About Cells, Bones, Muscles, and Joints
Michelle O'Brien-Palmer
This science activity book explores bones, muscles, joints, and other connective tissues and the amazing cells they are made of. A "growth portfolio" allows young scientists to track their growth, and silly songs and lively illustrations help them remember new words and concepts. All 60 activities have been tested in homes and classrooms to be sure they are safe, effective, and fun.
ages 5—9
ISBN 1-55652-367-X
128 pages, paper, $12.95

The Wind at Work
An Activity Guide to Windmills
Gretchen Woelfle
With more than a dozen wind-related activities and more than 100 photos, line drawings, charts, and graphs, this book traces the history of windmills and how their design and function have changed over time.
ages 8—13
ISBN 1-55652-308-4
144 pages, paper, $14.95

Women Invent
Two Centuries of Discoveries That Have Shaped Our World
Susan Casey
These inspiring stories of women inventors take the reader through the process of inventing—from coming up with an idea to having it manufactured and sold.
ages 9—13
ISBN 1-55652-317-3
144 pages, paper, $14.95

These books are available through your local bookstore or directly from Independent Publishers Group, 814 N. Franklin Street, Chicago, Illinois, 60610, 1-800-888-4741. Visa and MasterCard accepted.

978
CAR   Carlson, Laurie M.

           Westward ho!

DUE DATE	BRODART	12/05	14.95

Somerset Valley
School Library
45 Blake St
Hartland, Maine